understanding history 2

BLACKPOOL

Health & Pleasure, Glorious Sea

Through Bookings from the Principal Stations on the

MIDLAND RAILWAY.
Official Guide, with Map, &c., to be had at the RAILWAY BOOKSTALLS throughout England.

JOHN CHILD   TIM HODGE   PAUL SHUTER   DAVID TAYLOR

SERIES EDITOR: JOHN CHILD

HEINEMANN
EDUCATIONAL

Contents

1.1 Faith and Reason

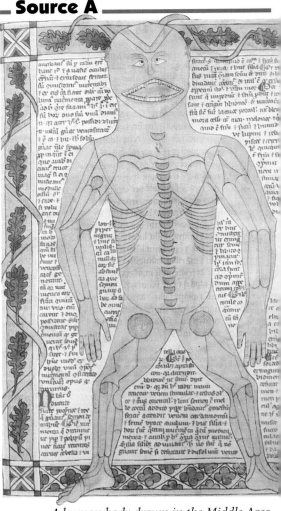

A human body drawn in the Middle Ages.

Renaissance means 'rebirth'. It is the name given to the period in Europe from about 1450 to 1650. During this time there was a growing interest in the ideas of the ancient Greeks and Romans. Some of the ideas, knowledge and skills of the Greeks and Romans had been lost or forgotten during the Dark Ages. In painting, sculpture and architecture these ideas were now reborn. The work of 15th and 16th-century artists like **Leonardo da Vinci, Michelangelo** and **Titian** is evidence of this rebirth.

These works of art show us that attitudes were changing. In the Middle Ages it was mainly priests who were involved in study and learning. Ordinary people were more prepared to accept that events could be explained simply as God's work. They did not try to work out new explanations. They accepted the teachings of the Church; they did not question them. In the Renaissance, study and learning were part of the lives of many people who were not churchmen. Many exciting 'new' ideas were recovered from the writings of the Greeks and Romans. Now, the simplistic drawings of the Middle Ages were not good enough. People wanted to see things as they really were. Simple explanations were not good enough either. They asked questions and wanted convincing answers. They wanted to know why things worked, and there were many who were trying to work out answers.

Printing played a big part in the spread of the new knowledge. In the Middle Ages books were copied by hand, and any illustrations were drawn or painted in them. Printed books could be produced much more quickly. They could also be illustrated with woodcuts like Source F. It was now possible to have many copies of a book, and have them quicker and cheaper than they would have been in the Middle Ages.

Nothing could be quite the same again. Not even religion could escape the desire to question old beliefs. The Church would find it difficult to answer the many questions people were now prepared to ask about its power, its wealth and its right to speak the word of God.

Pages from 'The Book of Hours', hand-written during the Middle Ages, before the invention of printing.

Source C

Leonardo's drawing of a human figure, late 15th century.

Source F

Prelum
Afcefianū

A printing press, 1520. This is a woodcut illustration from an early printed book.

Source D

This century, like a golden age, has restored to light the arts, which almost disappeared; poetry, painting, sculpture, architecture and music. We are achieving what was honoured among the ancient people, but which has been almost forgotten since then.

Marsilio Fincino, a writer from the Italian town of Florence, 1492.

Source E

I believe I can give you as complete satisfaction as anyone else in the construction of buildings both public and private, and in conducting water from one place to another. I can further execute sculpture in marble, bronze or clay. Also in painting I can do as much as anyone else, whoever he may be.

Leonardo's letter offering his services to Lodovico Sforza, ruler of Milan, 1483.

Questions

Section A

1 Using the sources, explain the meaning of the word 'Renaissance'.

2 Why was printing important in the Renaissance?

3 What are the main differences between Source A and Source C?

4 Who are the 'ancient people' referred to in Source D?

Section B

5 What differences are there between the illustration in Source B and Source F?

6 Look at Sources B and F. What do they tell you about the production of books?

7 Is Source C more useful than Source E as evidence of Leonardo's abilities? Explain your answer carefully.

1.2 The Catholic Church

In 1500 the **Catholic Church** was more than just a building to the people of Europe. It was a complete organization. It had cardinals, bishops, monks, nuns and priests, and the **Pope** in **Rome** as its leader. It looked after the body as well as the soul. The Church provided schools and hospitals, and cared for the old, the sick and the needy. It collected its own taxes and even had its own laws, **canon law.**

Many people still had a simple belief in God. They believed that if they led good lives and obeyed the Church's teaching they would go to heaven. If not, they would go to hell. Death was so common – with so much war and disease – and life was so hard, that people needed the comfort of God. The Church was the link between people and God. Most people's only contact with the Church was their local priest, so they looked to him for help and guidance.

However, all was not well with the Church. Kings and princes did not like the Pope making the laws in their lands. Some popes seemed more interested in their own power and wealth than in saving souls. Julius II (Pope 1503–13) even led an army into battle. The Renaissance encouraged people to think for themselves. They wondered why the Church was so wealthy and yet still asked them for money. They noticed that many priests and monks seemed more interested in their own pleasure than in caring for the people. Some questioned the practice of honouring **relics** (such as supposed bones of saints and splinters of the Cross). They had faith in God; but many were losing faith in the Church.

Source A

Education, in the sense of book-learning, was almost entirely in the hands of the Church in the Middle Ages. Teachers were nearly all monks, friars and priests – men who had taken 'holy orders'. Religion and education were so closely linked that if a man was called a clerk it meant both that he was a churchman and that he could read and write.

From R. J. Cootes, 'The Middle Ages', 1972.

Source B

Leo X (Pope 1513–21) by Raphael (1483–1520).

Source C

O Lord my God, how false are those who seem so spiritual. Their study is not to show God's works but to conceal the Devil's works. All is outward show, and there is no truth; nothing else but dung buried under snow; outside is the glistering whiteness of righteousness and honesty, inside a conscience reeking with vermin and with the stench of sin.

A preacher in Strasbourg Cathedral at the end of the 15th century.

Source D

'Dante and the Heavenly City' by Dominico de Michelino in the mid-15th century.

Source E

'Clothing the naked', one of the responsibilities of the Church, shown in a 16th-century sculpture.

Questions

Section A

1 List the reasons why the Church was so powerful in 1500.

2 a What is happening in Source D?
  b In what ways does Source D help to explain people's beliefs at the time?

3 List all the things people might have liked and disliked about the Church.

Section B

4 a Why might some people have wanted to honour and obtain relics?
  b Why might others have been suspicious of anyone selling relics?

5 What differences are there between churches in Britain today and the Catholic Church in 1500?

1.3 Europe and the Holy Roman Empire

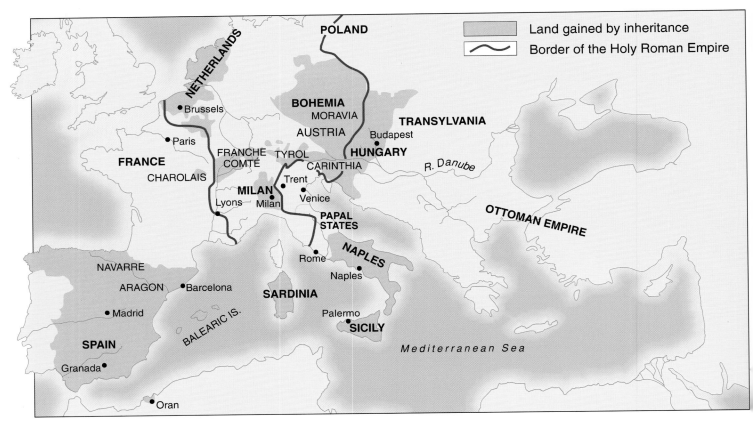

The Empire of Charles V.

Europe in 1519 was very different from the Europe of today. People did not always think of themselves as belonging to a nation. Italy and Germany did not exist as countries with clear borders. They were divided into areas run by local rulers. These rulers might be princes, bishops, archbishops, dukes or Electors. The areas we call Germany and Austria were part of the **Holy Roman Empire**. Although there was an emperor (chosen by the rulers called Electors), he didn't have much power over the states that made up his Empire. It was not really Roman at all, but rulers liked to think that it was the successor to the Roman Empire. Most people's strongest loyalty was to their local area and its ruler.

Power was gained by claiming and owning land and territory. Disputes over land often led to wars and, with territory changing hands, borders were not fixed for long. Even the Pope, who claimed leadership of all the Christian people of Europe, held territory like any other prince, called the **Papal States.**

Source A

In 1519 Charles defeated Francis I of France in the election for the imperial title. While the general distrust of France had gravely handicapped Francis, the election of Charles was not so much a manifestation of German nationalism – Charles was hardly more German than his rival – as the result of the superior military and financial position of the Hapsburgs in Germany.

From H.G.Koenigsberger and George L.Mosse, 'Europe in the Sixteenth Century', 1981.

Territory was treated as personal property to be passed on to the next generation by inheritance. To be accepted as head of a family was very important. Henry VIII was most concerned to produce a male heir to pass on his Tudor inheritance of England, Wales and Ireland. **Francis I** of the family of **Valois** controlled most of what is now France through his inheritance. Both Henry and Francis were clearly kings of England and France, but this kind of title could not be given to someone who inherited territory scattered all over Europe.

Charles of the **Hapsburg** family inherited such scattered lands. By 1519, he was the ruler of territory as far apart as Holland, Spain, Sicily and Naples as well as parts of Austria and Germany. It would be difficult to hold together these lands made up of so many different peoples. His chance came when he put his name forward for election as Holy Roman Emperor. This title would help him to claim leadership of Christian Europe and hold his Hapsburg inheritance together.

This is why Francis I also stood for election. If he lost to Charles his claims to territory would be threatened. By tradition, the title was decided by an odd assortment of German princes and archbishops, who together numbered just seven Electors. This was their opportunity to make money. Both candidates were prepared to spend huge sums of money to bribe the Electors. This gave Charles an advantage; with the backing of the banking house of Jacob Fugger he spent 850,000 florins in bribes. The Electors were also influenced by the feeling that Charles would not be as unpopular a choice with the German people as Francis. When the result was announced all seven Electors had voted for Charles. He was now the Holy Roman Emperor Charles V.

Source B

Jacob Fugger, painted about 1520.

Source C

The Emperor Charles V as a young man.

Questions

Section A

1 What was the Holy Roman Empire?

2 In what way was the Pope like other princes?

3 What are the main differences between Europe in 1519 and Europe today?

Section B

4 Why did both Francis and Charles want to be the Holy Roman Emperor?

5 For what reasons did the Electors all vote for Charles?

6 Do you think Charles could now rely on the loyalty of the German people? Give reasons for your answer.

1.4 Critics of the Church

We have already noted in Unit 1.2 the power of the Church and some of the reasons why people complained about it. This was nothing new. Some people had criticized the Church in public before 1500; others grumbled in private.

Openly criticizing the Church involved great risks. The Church said that only it could decide God's word. Anyone who openly disagreed with the Church's ideas could be accused of **heresy** and tried in the Church court. If convicted, the sentence was death by burning at the stake. The rest of this unit tells you about the fate of four people during the Middle Ages who criticized the Church.

In 1377 **John Wyclif**, a teacher at Oxford University, was called before the Archbishop of Canterbury to answer for his views. Wyclif argued that no Pope could be more important than God. Christians should not obey any churchman who lived a life of luxury. Monks and bishops should give up their riches and lead simple lives. Wyclif had the Bible translated into English, so that people could read God's word for themselves.

Wyclif died before he could be punished by the Church, but his followers, known as **Lollards**, were silenced by the Church and burned at the stake. Wyclif's body was dug up, burned and thrown in a river. **John Huss** of Bohemia expresssed similar views; in 1415 he was burned at the stake.

Sometimes even those who were loyal to the Church were accused of heresy and sentenced to death. In 1431 **Joan of Arc**, who had led France to victory in battle against the English, was accused and burned at the stake. Despite her success, a French Church court sentenced her to death. She had offended powerful men by wearing soldier's armour in battle and claiming to hear the voice of God and the saints telling her what to do. She was only 19 years old when she died.

Girolamo Savonarola tried to persuade the people of Florence to become more religious. When the King of France invaded Italy, Savonarola claimed it was a punishment from God for their wickedness. People were convinced by Savonarola and for a time they helped him attack luxury and wickedness. But the Pope was not pleased. He lived a very luxurious life. When Savonarola refused to stop preaching he was expelled from the Church. The people of Florence turned against him and he too was burned at the stake in 1498.

Source A

When she was brought out, and saw the horrible apparatus of death, her fortitude failed her, and she was led, struggling and sobbing, to the stake. When she saw the fire kindled, she grasped a crucifix and called loudly on the Almighty for support. She was thus seen, when the dense smoke enveloped her, praying fervently to Christ for mercy.

The death of Joan of Arc. From 'Cassell's Illustrated History of England', 1873.

Source B

Not the Pope, but Christ only is the head; and not the cardinals, but all Christ's faithful people be the body of the Catholic Church. If the Pope be a reprobate [immoral person], it is plain that he is no head, no nor member even, of the Holy Church of God, but of the Devil.

John Huss quoted in 'Foxe's Book of Martyrs', first published in 1559. This version was published in 1965.

Source C

There was never so much religion and virtue in Florence as in Savonarola's day. The taverns were closed, women dressed modestly, and children lived a life of holiness.

From C. R. N. Routh, 'They Saw it Happen in Europe, 1450–1600', 1965.

Source D

Savonarola being burned in the square at Florence, 1498. This is an anonymous painting, thought to have been made shortly after Savonarola's execution.

Questions

Section A

1 Explain in your own words the meaning of the word **heresy**.

2 Joan of Arc claimed that she could hear the saints and God talking to her directly. Why might this have angered the Church?

3 What were the Church's objections to:
 a Wyclif, **b** Huss, **c** Savonarola?

4 Study Source D.
 a Is there anything to show that Savonarola is being executed for a religous crime?
 b Is this a realistic picture?
 c The burning of Savonarola was watched by a huge crowd. Does this mean that this painting is of no use to historians? Give reasons for your answer.

Section B

5 Why was Wyclif's body dug up, burned and thrown into a river?

6 Joan of Arc, Huss and Savonarola were all put to death for **heresy**. Does this mean that the **causes** of their executions must all have been religious? Explain your answer.

1.5 Martin Luther

The start of the 16th century was a difficult time in Europe. Poor peasants were suffering from high prices and low wages. Kings, princes and the Holy Roman Emperor all wanted more control over their territories. Nowhere was the atmosphere more tense than in **Germany**. Here, the anger and resentment against the power and influence of the Pope and the Church were felt especially strongly. The German **Diet** (a type of parliament) regularly received thousands of complaints about the Church from people of all classes.

In 1517 a monk and teacher of religion, **Martin Luther**, wrote a list of complaints about the Church. These complaints later became known as the **Ninety-Five Theses**. He decided to write them when Johann Tetzel arrived near Wittenberg, where Luther was teaching. Tetzel had been sent to sell **indulgences** for the Pope and the Archbishop of Mainz. People who bought indulgences were told that this would buy them pardons for their sins, not just for the living but also for the dead. They were told that their souls would spend less time in **purgatory**. This was where the Church said the souls of the dead went to be punished for sins before going to heaven.

Source A

Johann Tetzel collecting money for 'indulgences', with the help of Fugger bankers, 1517.

Source B

God, Luther claimed, would pardon all who believed in Christ, whether or not they did kind deeds, or attended masses. 'Good works will never make a good man, but a good man does good works,' he explained. A man's only hope was to have faith. This alone could lead to salvation.

From L. E. Snellgrove, 'The Early Modern Age', 1972.

Source C

Unless I am convicted by Scripture and plain reason (for I do not accept the authority of popes and councils, since they have often erred and contradicted each other), my conscience is captive to the word of God. I cannot and I will not recant anything, for to go against conscience is neither right nor safe. God help me. Amen.

Martin Luther at the Diet of Worms, 1521.

Source D

Martin Luther (1483–1546), painted by Cranach the Younger (1472–1553).

Source E

A woodcut by Cranach the Younger, about 1540, showing Luther in the pulpit. Luther is pointing out the right way to celebrate devotion to Christ – and the fate of his opponents.

It seemed to Luther that the Pope and the Church had reduced religion to a product to be sold. The Pope wanted the money to help build a splendid new church of St. Peter in Rome. Also, Church officials were allowed to buy their positions – a practice called **simony**. The Archbishop of Mainz had borrowed money to become Archbishop, and now needed money to repay his debts.

Luther's writings were soon being read all over Germany. He wanted a **pure** and **simple religion** and challenged the whole basis of the power of the Catholic Church. There was no need for Pope or priests, he said; monasteries should be closed and priests be allowed to marry. He also said that the bread and wine did not actually turn into the body and blood of Christ during communion. Faith in God was enough to save souls. Luther's ideas attracted many followers, who became known as **Protestants.**

To the Pope this was heresy. Luther had to be silenced. In 1520 Luther was sent a **papal bull**, which condemned him and his beliefs. A bull is an official order from the Pope. Many people in Germany agreed with Luther, and with their support he publicly burned the bull. The new Holy Roman Emperor, Charles V, was a faithful Catholic and ruled Catholic lands, so he could not side with Luther. In 1521 he called Luther to answer for his views at the **Diet of Worms**. Luther went there and stood by his beliefs. With the two most powerful men in Europe against him, Luther was risking his life. He was given protection by Frederick, the Elector of Saxony. His protest was much more widely supported and could not be silenced. The **Protestant Reformation** had begun.

Source F

We can no longer suffer the serpent to creep through the field of the Lord. The books of Martin Luther which contain these errors are to be examined and burned.

From the papal bull of Pope Leo X, 1520.

Questions

Section A

1 a What were indulgences?
  b How did the Pope's and the Archbishop of Mainz's need for money make the Church more likely to upset Luther?

2 What happened at the Diet of Worms?

3 Why could the Emperor Charles V not afford to support Luther?

4 Make a list of all the complaints people made against the Church. (Use other units in Part 1 to help you.) Then design your own protest poster.

Section B

5 Study the following list carefully:
  ● the wealth and power of the Church
  ● complaints against the Church
  ● the protest of Martin Luther
  ● the support given to Luther by the German people
  ● the spread of his ideas with the invention of printing.
  a Were each of these factors **causes** of the Reformation? Give reasons for your answer.
  b Which factors are long-term and which are short-term causes of the Reformation?
  c Were all these causes equally important? Give reasons for your answer.

1.6 Divided by Religion

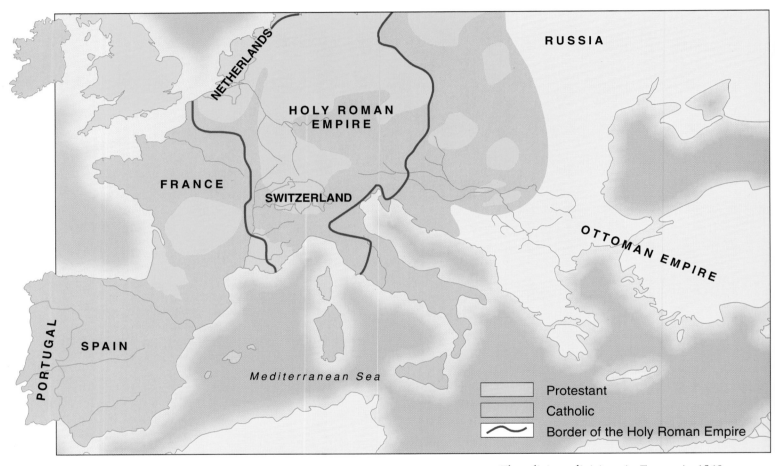

The religious divisions in Europe in 1560.

Martin Luther's protest led to great changes in Europe. As you can see from the map, many areas broke away from the Catholic Church. This was mainly in the **Holy Roman Empire** although the revolt spread to other parts of Europe as well. However, much of Europe stayed loyal to the Catholic Church. The idea of a Europe united by religion was gone forever.

It has been suggested that the Emperor Charles V might have kept the Empire together by leading the revolt himself. He was not prepared to do that. Instead, he stayed loyal to the Catholic faith and outlawed Luther. Still, there were many others prepared to join the revolt.

A message from Charles V to his subjects in 1521.

Source A

It is certain that a single monk must be wrong if he stands against the opinion of all Christendom. Otherwise Christendom itself would have been wrong for more than a thousand years. I have therefore resolved to stake upon this cause all my dominions, my friends, my body and my blood, my life and my soul. From now on I shall regard Luther as a notorious heretic and hope that you, as good Christians, will not be wanting in your duty.

Source B

> If the peasant is in open rebellion, then he is outside the law of God, for rebellion is not simply murder, but it is like a great fire which attacks and lays waste a whole land. Thus, rebellion brings with it a land full of murders and bloodshed, makes widows and orphans and turns everything upside down like a great disaster. Therefore, let everyone who can, smite, slay and stab, secretly or openly, remembering that nothing can be more poisonous, hurtful or devilish than a rebel.

From Martin Luther, 'Against the Murdering, Thieving Hordes of Peasants', 1525.

Luther had started something he could not control. He was embarrassed by some who used his name. Between 1524 and 1526 the Peasants' Revolt spread through southern Germany. To them, Luther stood for freedom and revolt against authority. Angered by high prices, lower wages and new laws, they attacked rich landowners and religious orders alike. Luther was horrified by this and wrote a pamphlet urging the revolt to be crushed.

Luther wanted a simple religion in which souls could be saved by faith in God. He believed that all people should be able to read the Bible and understand the Church service in their own language. But others went further than Luther had intended. Even in Wittenburg the Mass was abolished and mobs attacked churches and priests. The **Anabaptists** believed that only adults should be baptized. They preached that a true Christian could not sin and Christ would soon return to earth. The peasants had been roused by an Anabaptist, Thomas Müntzer, who preached that only the poor could be saved. In 1525 his army was defeated by a group of German princes and he was beheaded. Ten years later in the town of Münster, John of Leyden set up a 'holy community'. Money was not used in the town and everything was owned by the community. That, too, was crushed when Catholic troops entered the town and massacred the people.

Luther was caught between the Catholics and the extreme Protestants. He had to rely on the support of the princes and city councils. They could be free of the Emperor's control as members of Luther's Church. They could also keep the poor in order. Luther thought it was a sin for a subject to disobey his prince.

When Luther died in 1546 the Emperor Charles V was at war with the Protestant princes. Charles wanted to return the Empire to the Catholic faith. He had to accept failure. By the Peace of Augsburg (1555) it was agreed that each state must follow the religion of its ruler. In the next century another Emperor again tried to make the Empire Catholic. The result was the Thirty Years War during which ten million Germans died. Germany and much of Europe was still divided by religion.

Questions

Section A

1 a How important was it for Charles V to silence Martin Luther?
  b How successful was he?

2 a Did the peasants support Luther for religious reasons? Explain your answer carefully.
  b Why did Luther not support the Peasants' Revolt?

3 What were the main beliefs of the Anabaptists?

4 Copy the map.
  a Why might Protestantism have done better in the Holy Roman Empire than in France?
  b Does the map mean that there were no Catholics in England and no Protestants in Northern France in 1560?

Section B

5 How does the map help to show how some people changed their religion and some did not?

6 Did the changes in religion mean that Europe had made **progress** or had **regressed** from the time when everyone was Catholic? Explain your answer carefully.

1.7 *John Calvin*

A Catholic view of John Calvin (1509–64).

John Calvin was a French scholar of law and religion. He was driven out of France because of his religious beliefs. He settled near Geneva in Switzerland in 1541. Here he set up a religious group. As a reformer his influence was great. His ideas attracted many people from all over Europe to visit Geneva. Soon his followers set up similar churches in parts of France and Germany as well as Switzerland. Calvin's influence was particularly strong in the Netherlands and Scotland.

Calvin's ideas were partly based on Luther's, but in some ways followers of the two men could not agree. Just because they had broken with the Catholic Church did not mean that Protestants all shared the same beliefs. Calvin claimed that only God could decide who would be saved and who would not. Only those whom God had chosen before they were born would go to heaven. This led him to preach the idea of **predestination**. Calvin's followers believed they were the chosen ones: the **elect**.

Calvin believed strongly that a church must be organized and disciplined. He put forward his suggestions for church rules in a book, ***Institutes of Christian Religion.*** These ideas were put into practice in **Geneva**, which became a model religious community. Groups of preachers, teachers, elders and deacons ran the Church. All life in the city was strictly controlled by a governing body of church officials and townspeople called the **consistory**. The consistory made the laws and made sure they were obeyed. Under these arrangements, schools and hospitals were provided, and the poor were looked after. Even the streets were kept clean, and shopkeepers were expected to charge fair prices.

Discipline was strict in Geneva. The religious life was a serious business, and there was little place for pleasure or enjoyment. To some people the city was a place to be praised and copied. Others were horrified by the stories of what took place under the influence of John Calvin.

Calvin set out to spread his faith. Pastors were trained in Geneva and sent out to other places in Europe. **John Knox** of Scotland was one such pastor. He set up the Presbyterian Church in Scotland, based on the Calvinist faith. By the time of Calvin's death in 1564 there were Calvinist churches in France and the Netherlands as well as Scotland. England too was influenced by Calvinism.

From L. E. Snellgrove, 'The Early Modern Age', 1972.

It is little wonder that, in spite of all its imperfections, the small city of Geneva came to represent for Calvinists the godly society in working order.

From H. G. Koenigsberger and George L. Mosse, 'Europe in the 16th Century', 1968.

Consistory members patrolled the streets so that 'their eyes might be on the people'. Dancing and games were forbidden; hotels and inns were closed for a time. Theatres showed only religious plays. Laughing was frowned upon and non-Christian first names were condemned. Those who did wrong were tried by the consistory every week. Punishments varied from fines and penances to whipping and death. A girl who put irreligious words to a psalm was beaten. An important town councillor who dared to call Calvin a bad man was made to walk through the streets dressed only in a shirt and carrying a candle. A boy who struck his parents was beheaded.

This new form of Christianity appealed to many nationalities and types of people – from merchants in Switzerland to great landowners in Scotland. Many people joined to be saved; Calvinism seemed to offer that certainty. Others liked the order, harmony and discipline of Geneva. Calvin and his followers also preached the right of resistance to unfair or bad rulers. For people like the Dutch, this was another attraction.

Events in France

The **French** Calvinists became widespread and strong. They were known as **Huguenots**. They even tried to take over the French throne. There was a long civil war with the Catholics and many Huguenots were massacred. Finally, by the **Edict of Nantes** of 1598, the Huguenots were given religious freedom. The religious disputes died down for a time. However, the majority of French people stayed loyal to the Catholic Church.

Events in the Netherlands

The **Dutch** were ruled by the Catholic King of Spain at this time. They wanted their freedom and rebelled against the Spanish rulers and the Catholic Church. Their most famous leader was William of Orange. He was assassinated, but by 1600 the Dutch were independent and Calvinists.

Source D

You will hardly believe the influence which the principal minister of Geneva, by name Calvin, possesses in this kingdom. He is a man of extraordinary authority, who by his mode of life, his doctrines and his writings rises superior to all the rest. It is almost impossible to believe the enormous sums of money which are secretly sent to him to maintain his power.

A report from the Venetian Ambassador in France, 1561.

Source E

Geneva, where I neither fear man nor am ashamed to say that this is the most perfect school of Christ that ever was on the Earth since the days of the Apostles. In other places I confess Christ to be truly preached; but I have not yet seen in any other place manners and religion to be so sincerely reformed.

John Knox (1514–72), the Scots priest, expressing his admiration for Calvin's Geneva.

Source F

PROMPTE · ET · SINCERE ·

IOHANNES · CALVINVS ·
ANNO · ÆTATIS · 53 ·
· B ·

A stone memorial to John Calvin, made in 1553.

Questions

Section A

1 a How can you tell that the artist who drew Source A did not like Calvin?

   b Did the creator of Source F feel the same way towards Calvin as the creator of Source A? Explain your answer.

2 Explain in your own words the meaning of:
   ● the **elect**
   ● **predestination**
   ● **consistory**.

Section B

3 Study these two sentences: 'Calvin lived in Geneva'; 'Calvin was a cruel man'. Which is a **fact** and which is an **opinion**? Explain your answer.

4 a Sources B and C give different impressions of Geneva. Does this mean they contradict one another?

   b Which do you think is the better source?

2.1 The Tudor Period

The **Tudors** ruled England from 1485 to 1603. During the Tudor period the **population of England** rose from about 3.5 million to 5 million. Only about one-tenth of these people lived in towns. London was the biggest town. Its population increased from 60,000 in 1500 to 250,000 in 1600. Other important towns included York, Bristol, Norwich and Newcastle, each with about 10,000 people. Most people lived in small villages in the countryside. Much of the countryside was heavily forested.

Farming was the main occupation in Tudor times. Most people grew just enough food for themselves. But during the 16th century, farmers began to **enclose** their land, rather than having it in small strips. They joined the strips together to make fields. This made their farming more efficient and they could produce more food to sell in the growing towns.

In 1536 Henry VIII **closed down the monasteries** and sold off their land. Wool prices were high, so people bought up the monastic lands very quickly and enclosed them in order to keep sheep.

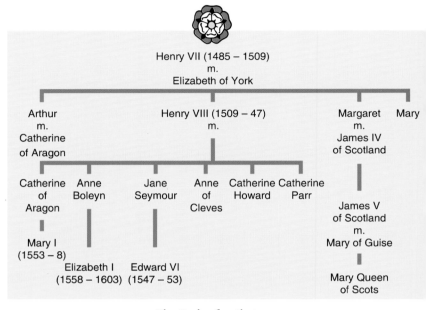

The Tudor family tree.

Foreign lands discovered during the Tudor period.

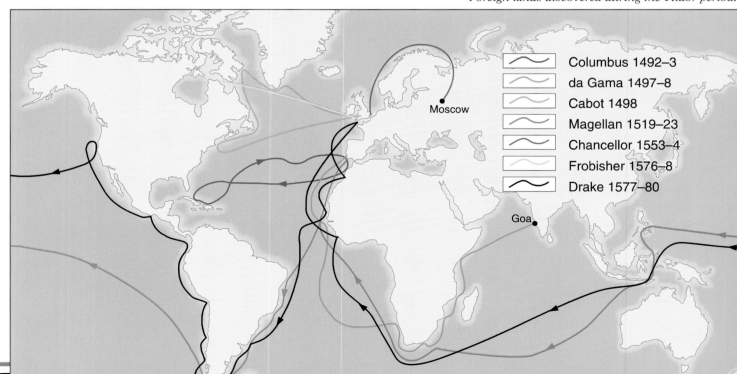

Source A

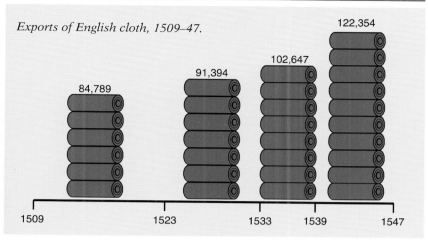

Exports of English cloth, 1509–47.

84,789 — 1509
91,394 — 1523
102,647 — 1533/1539
122,354 — 1547

Industry also grew during the Tudor period. The making of woollen cloth was most important, with East Anglia, the West Country and West Yorkshire being the main regions. Coal and tin mining, iron smelting, cannon making and shipbuilding were also important occupations. With the discovery of **gunpowder** there was a change in warfare. Wars were now fought with guns, although archers were still used in many battles. Much stronger and bigger ships were now needed to resist cannon fire.

A feature of the 16th century was a general **rise in prices**. The poor were badly affected by this and poverty increased during this period. But merchants made bigger profits from the higher prices.

Between 1529 and 1536 **Henry VIII** quarrelled with the Pope. This led to Henry breaking away from the Catholic Church and setting up the **Church of England**. England became a Protestant country. This was the **English Reformation**. The Reformation had started in Europe in 1517 when Martin Luther questioned the teachings of the Catholic Church. This was a brave thing to do as the Catholic Church was very powerful (see Unit 1.5).

By the middle of the 16th century, the ideas of the **Renaissance** also began to spread to England. People started to observe, experiment and think scientifically (see Unit 1.1). This led people to question many old ideas which had been upheld by the Church. For example, in 1543 **Nicholas Copernicus** said that the Earth revolved around the Sun (the Church said the Earth was the centre of the universe). The new ideas were spread in books which were mass-produced on the new **printing presses**. People became more curious and started to think for themselves rather than just believe what the Church said.

Europeans increased their knowledge of the world during the 16th century. They found new lands and sometimes conquered them. Spain had the greatest success, but English merchants often traded with the Spanish colonies.

Source B

Sheep farming became more important during Tudor times. This illustration was published at the end of the Tudor period.

Questions

Section A

1 Draw a **timeline** which shows the length of the reign of each Tudor monarch. Make 1 mm equal 1 year on your timeline.

2 Study Source B. How does this source help to explain why many farm workers were unemployed in the Tudor period?

3 Using an atlas, find out the names of the places visited by each explorer shown on the map.

Section B

5 Make a presentation on a large piece of paper called 'Aspects of Life in the Tudor Period'. Use the following headings:
- the Reformation
- occupations
- population
- the Renaissance
- the New World.

Use writing, maps, diagrams and pictures in your presentation. Make sure you include labels and captions.

6 Are any of the headings in question **5** connected in any way? Explain your answer.

2.2 Henry VII Restores Order

Name	Reigned	
	From	To
Edward III	1327	1377
Richard II	1377	1399
Henry IV	1399	1413
Henry V	1413	1422
Henry VI	1422	1461
Edward IV	1461	1483
Edward V	1483	1483
Richard III	1483	1485

Kings of England who reigned before Henry VII.

In August 1485, **Henry Tudor** (of the house of Lancaster) was crowned **King Henry VII** of England.

On 18 January 1486 Henry married **Elizabeth** (of the House of York), the daughter of Edward IV. Despite the union of the two houses, there were many attempts by the Yorkists to throw Henry off the throne. They believed that Henry had no right to be the king. Henry survived all these attempts. Many historians say that Henry VII's reign ended the Middle Ages and started modern times. They argue that this was so because Henry introduced lots of new ways of governing and keeping law and order. Others say that the only thing that changed in 1485 was the king; everything else stayed the same.

During the Wars of the Roses a number of barons had built up large private armies. Henry feared that these might be used against him. The **Act of Livery and Maintenance** (1487), which copied an earlier Act of 1468, banned these armies. Any baron who disobeyed this law was brought to London and tried by the **Court of the Star Chamber**. This court was made of members of the king's council. Barons who were found guilty were heavily fined. Poor people could take their complaints to the **Court of Requests**, which had been set up in 1483 by Richard III. Henry VII thought that a court where the poor could get legal help was a good idea and should be maintained.

For the most part Henry ran the government himself, together with his council of ministers. His council was made up of trusted nobles and bishops. Like other kings before him, Henry VII summoned **Parliament** only when he needed it. The main purpose of calling a Parliament was to vote in new taxes (usually to pay for a war) or to approve new laws. Parliament was called on just seven occasions between 1485 and 1509. Like Edward IV and Richard III, Henry appointed a Speaker to keep control of the House of Commons.

Source A

Marriage alliances had been used since Anglo-Saxon times. The promotion of trade had been important since the merchant class grew up in the 14th century.

From A. R. Myers, 'England in the Late Middle Ages (1377–1536)', 1952.

Source B

Portrait of Henry VII painted in 1504 by Michel Sittow. Henry's wife, Elizabeth of York, had died in 1503 and he was hoping to marry again in order to make England more powerful in Europe.

Source C

A gilt bronze effigy of Henry and Elizabeth in Westminster Abbey. This was erected according to instructions Henry left in his will. The monument was completed in 1518 by Thomas Duchemann.

Councils were used to govern remote parts of England. Henry brought back the **Council of the Marches** to keep Wales under control. This council had first been used by Edward IV. Later, Henry introduced councils to govern the North of England, Devon and Cornwall. Law and order on a local level continued to be looked after by **Justices of the Peace** (first introduced by Edward III).

When Henry became king the **Royal Treasury** was almost empty. He raised money by asking the barons for 'gifts' and by making them pay taxes which had been written into the Magna Carta of 1215. For example, if a baron's eldest son was knighted, or if his eldest daughter got married, a tax was due to the king. Like Edward IV, Henry was also very strict in collecting the rents from the royal estates and he also obtained money by taxing wool exports and foreign goods coming into England.

Henry was anxious to avoid **costly wars**. In 24 years he fought just one war. This was against France in 1491. It lasted three weeks and Henry was able to make a profit from it! This was because Parliament granted more money than was actually needed, and the French paid Henry to end the war. To keep the peace with other countries, Henry used marriages. Arthur, his eldest son, was married to a Spanish princess, **Catherine of Aragon,** in 1498. Then, in 1503, Margaret, his eldest daughter, was married to **James IV of Scotland**. Henry also made trading agreements with Spain and the Netherlands.

Source D

When Henry died, he left his son a secure throne, loyal barons and wealth: everything he had lacked in 1485.

From David Kennedy, 'Tudors and Stuarts', 1981.

Questions

Section A

1 Do you think Source B is reliable? Explain your answer.

2 'Monuments such as Source C are not very useful to historians.' Do you agree or disagree with this statement? Give reasons for your answer.

Section B.

3 a Copy and complete the chart below:

Methods of government used by Henry VII and reasons		
	Old or new method	Henry's reasons
Court of Star Chamber		
Court of Requests		
Use of Parliament		
Raising money		
Foreign relations		

b Shade in different colours those methods which were new and those which were old.

c 'Henry VII introduced hardly anything which was new in the methods he used to rule England.' Do you agree or disagree? Give reasons for your answer.

4 Did Henry change anything at all? Explain your answer.

2.3 Henry VIII and the English Reformation

At first **Martin Luther**'s quarrel with the Pope did not affect England much. But relations between the Pope and **Henry VIII** became worse during the late 1520s and early 1530s.

In 1533 and 1534 Henry broke away from the Catholic Church. He set up his own Church by a series of Acts of Parliament. In 1536, he **dissolved** (closed down) the smaller monasteries. In 1539, he dissolved the remaining monasteries and published a version of the Bible in English.

Some people were so horrified by what Henry had done that they rebelled against him. Others were burned at the stake rather than give up their old Catholic religion.

Historians have been keen to explain the causes of such important events, but they have not always agreed with each other about what those causes were. This unit looks at four different factors which may have helped cause the 'English Reformation'.

Theology

The **theology** of a religion is the collection of its most important beliefs. Martin Luther was not the first person to criticize the ideas of the Catholic Church, but his criticisms found many supporters. His most important criticism was that the Catholic Church had changed from the way the early Church was organized in the Bible. He also criticized the power of the Pope and the luxurious lives led by some churchmen. Protestants believed that the Bible should be the basis of all Christian faith and that as many people as possible should be able to read the Bible in their own language.

Source A

An official painting of Henry VIII, Jane Seymour, his third queen, and their son, who later became King Edward VI. Henry married Catherine of Aragon (his brother's widow) in 1509, but divorced her in 1533 to marry Anne Boleyn. He had Anne executed in 1536. They had one daughter, Elizabeth. Next, still in 1536, Henry married Jane Seymour. She died in 1537 following the birth of a son, Edward. In 1540 Henry married Anne of Cleves, but the marriage was annulled the same year. Later that year he married Catherine Howard, who was executed in 1542. Finally, in 1543 he married Catherine Parr. She married again after Henry's death in 1547.

Divorce

Henry VIII wanted to have a **son** to follow him as king. One of the most important things a king had to do, people believed, was to make sure there was at least one healthy son to inherit the throne. To be on the safe side it was considered a good idea to have more than one son. (Henry's own elder brother, Arthur, had died aged 15.) This wasn't just a matter of fathers wanting sons. Most people believed then that only a man could control the powerful nobles. To have no children, or to have only daughters, meant there was a great risk of **civil war** breaking out after the king's death.

In 1527 Henry VIII had two problems. Catherine of Aragon, his wife since 1509, was too old to have any more children, and only one of their children, a girl called Mary, had lived. The second problem was that Anne Boleyn, whom Henry was attracted to, had refused to become his mistress and insisted that he would have to marry her. He decided that for the sake of the country he would divorce Queen Catherine and marry again so that he could have sons.

Under the Catholic Church only the Pope could grant a divorce. Between 1527 and 1529 Henry tried to get the Pope to agree to a divorce for him, but he refused. Henry continued to look for ways to change the Pope's mind until, in 1533, he had the Archbishop of Canterbury grant him a divorce – against the Pope's wishes.

Money

Henry VIII had been involved in a number of **wars in Europe**, all of which had been expensive. He could not raise enough money by taxes and was always looking for extra sources of money. In 1535 Henry ordered an investigation into the **wealth of the monasteries**. This showed that the monasteries owned about one-quarter of the land in England.

Unpopularity of the Church

The Catholic Church was unpopular with many people. It was felt that the Church was interested in money more than in faith. Monks and nuns came in for special criticism, because many people felt that rather than living pure and simple lives, as they should, they were living in luxury and were corrupt. Henry's investigation of the monasteries in 1535 produced many reports like this one: 'The prior a very virtuous man, but his monks more corrupt than any others in vices. Some monks have ten women, some eight.'

Questions

Section A

1 Draw a **timeline** covering the years 1509 to 1547. Mark on it:
 a the most important events of the Reformation in Europe (see Part One).
 b the events in the English Reformation mentioned in this unit.
 c Henry VIII's marriages.

2 What were the main theological criticisms of the Catholic Church?

3 Why did Henry VIII feel he needed a son?

4 Why was Henry's divorce a religious problem?

5 Why did Henry need money?

6 How did Henry know about the wealth of the Catholic Church?

7 a Why was the Catholic Church unpopular in England?
 b Do you think the Catholic Church was unpopular with everyone in England?

8 a Source A is an 'impossible picture'. Why?
 b Does this mean Source A cannot tell historians anything useful? Explain your answer.

Section B

9 The key events in the English Reformation happened in 1533. Does this mean **divorce** was the only real cause?

10 Is it possible to say that one (or more) of the English Reformation's four causes was a **short-term cause** and the others were **long-term causes**? Give reasons for your answer.

11 Do you think one of the causes was more important than the others? If so, which? If not, why not? Explain your answer.

2.4 Religion in the Reign of Edward VI

Source A

A painting with a political message. Edward VI is seated on the throne, with his council seated at the table. The Pope is wearing the pointed hat. This painting is by an unknown artist, 1548–49.

When Henry VIII died, his son, **Edward**, became king. Edward was only nine years old. He could not rule the country himself. Most of the work usually done by the king was done by one of Edward's uncles, the **Duke of Somerset**. Somerset was a Protestant who thought that the changes made in the Church after the Reformation had not gone far enough. With the support of the young king he set about making England a more Protestant country.

In the 16th century, England was a Christian country. There were no people of other faiths, and very few people who did not believe in God at all. People believed in heaven and hell. They felt that those who did not live proper Christian lives would go to hell, a place of everlasting torture and torment.

Activities

Study Source A.

1 Who is in the bed?

2 Who are the people at the bottom on the left, and what is happening to them?

3 What is happening out of the window?

At this time Christians believed that the **way** they worshipped God was important. They believed that if they worshipped God in the wrong way they would be likely to go to hell rather than heaven. Until the Reformation all people in England had worshipped in the same way, the way of the Catholic Church. After the Reformation the church services were changed a little, but they were still very similar to the old services.

Catholics believed that the Pope should be head of the Church, and that religion should be based both on what the Pope said and what the Bible said. They held their services in Latin, with the priest dressed in splendid and costly robes. Churches were decorated with paintings, stained-glass windows and statues of saints and the Virgin Mary. The altar was in the east.

Protestants believed that religion should be based on the Bible. They wanted nothing to do with the Pope. They wanted services in English, with the priest dressed in plain and simple robes. They also thought that churches should be as plain and simple as possible, without any paintings or statues.

After the Reformation, Henry VIII had made the churches hold their services in English; but he did not change anything else. Now the Duke of Somerset and Edward VI made the following changes to the English Church to make it more Protestant:

● **1547** Statues and pictures were removed from churches.
● **1547** A book of Protestant sermons was printed which had to be read in all churches.
● **1549** A prayer book was introduced with new services for all churches. The changes included moving the altar to the centre of the church, plain clothes for the priest and an end to parts of the service that were just English translations of the old Catholic services.

Source B

A 16th-century view of hell.

Questions

Section A

1 Copy out the following paragraph, choosing the better alternative from the words in *italics*.

In the 16th century all *Christians/Catholics* believed in hell. They believed that if they did not worship God *every Sunday/in the right way* they would go to hell when they died. This meant that the way church services were held mattered *both to Catholics and to Protestants/only to Protestants* very much.

2 What is happening to the people in hell in Source B?

Section B

3 How do you think people who preferred the Catholic style of church service would have felt about the changes in Edward VI's reign?

4 In 1549 there was a rebellion in Devon and Cornwall against Edward VI. Here is an extract from the demands of the rebels:

'We will have the mass [service] in Latin, as was before. Images [pictures and statues] to be set up again in every church.'

How do you think people in the rest of England would have felt about the rebellion and the demands of the rebels?

5 Do you think Source A was painted by a Protestant or a Catholic? Give reasons for your answer.

2.5 The Reign of Mary I

Queen Mary I was the eldest daughter of Henry VIII. She became queen in 1533 after her brother Edward VI died. Straight away she changed the way the English Church was run, making it much more like the old Catholic Church. Next, in 1554 she married King Philip of Spain. Spain was one of the most powerful countries in Europe, and one of the most Catholic. There was a revolt in England against Mary and her marriage, but it was easily defeated.

In November 1554 Mary and her new husband made England part of the Catholic Church again. The following year Mary began the **persecution of the Protestants**. People who would not rejoin the Catholic Church and accept the Pope as its head were imprisoned and sometimes tortured. If they still refused, they were burned at the stake. Between 1555 and 1558, when Mary died, about 280 people were burned. Some of the bishops who had been the leaders of the Church during Edward VI's reign were burned. Most of those killed this way, however, were poor men and women who could not afford to leave the country.

Source B

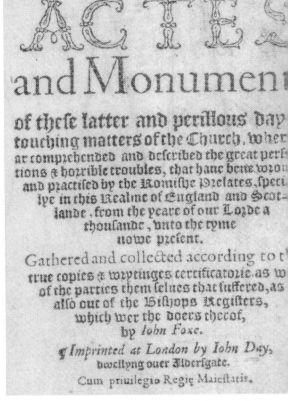

Part of the title page from the 1563 edition of Foxe's 'Book of Martyrs'.

Source C

Then the reeds being set about him, Wade made a hole by his face, that his voice might be heard. His tormentors cast the faggots [bundles of straw] at the same hole, his face being hurt with the end of a faggot cast thereat. The fire being put unto him, he cried unto God often: 'Lord Jesus! Receive my soul,' still holding his hands up over his head together towards heaven, even when he was dead and altogether roasted.

Christopher Wade, a weaver, was burned at the stake for refusing to give up his Protestantism. From Foxe's 'Book of Martyrs'.

Source A

The burning of Latimer and Ridley, two of Edward VI's bishops. The picture is taken from Foxe's 'Book of Martyrs'.

Source D

The story of the people who were burned during Mary's reign was told in a very famous book written at the time. Its author, **John Foxe**, was a Protestant who escaped abroad during the persecution. The book has a very long title (as you can see from Source B); it is usually called Foxe's **Book of Martyrs**. This was the second most popular book in England for the next 100 years (the most popular was the Bible). Many people in Tudor England could not read, but books were read out loud and the pictures could be seen by all.

Bishop Bonner, one of Mary's Catholic bishops, whipping a Protestant in the garden of the bishop's palace. Picture taken from Foxe's 'Book of Martyrs'.

Questions

Section A

1 Draw a **timeline** showing the events of Mary's reign mentioned in this unit.

2 Mary changed England's religion in two stages.
  a What was the first change?
  b What was the second change?
  c Why do you think she split the changes up like this?

3 Many 16th-century rulers persecuted people who did not agree with their religious ideas. Yet Mary has a reputation for being a fanatic. Why do you think this is?

4 Making out the words of older documents can sometimes be a problem. Copy out the words from the title page of Foxe's *Book of Martyrs*.

Section B

5 a Does Source B suggest Foxe might have been biased in any way? Quote from the source to support your answer.
  b Does your answer fit in with what the text tells you about Foxe's life? Give reasons for your answer.
  c Does this mean historians should not use Foxe's *Book of Martyrs* as a source when studying the reign of Queen Mary?

6 Copy the following statements. In each case say whether you think the sources in this unit prove that the statement is **true** or **false**, or that you **can't be sure**. Explain your reasons.
  a 'Some Protestants were cruelly treated during Mary's reign.'
  b 'All Protestants were badly treated during Mary's reign.'
  c 'Foxe did not like the way the Catholics acted during Mary's reign.'

7 Source C is a written source while Source A is a drawing. Does this mean that Source C is more likely to be reliable?

3.1 The Counter-Reformation

The Catholic Church reformed itself in the 16th century. This is called the **Counter-Reformation.** It started before Luther's revolt. However, by about 1550 there was an urgent need to do more to prevent the whole of Europe becoming Protestant. By 1650 the spread of Protestantism had slowed down and some areas had been won back by the Catholic Church.

There was a lot to put right in the Catholic Church. The Church seemed too distant from the lives of ordinary men and women. From the Pope down, churchmen seemed interested only in worldly wealth and power. Local priests often lacked the ability to do their jobs. Bishops rewarded their relatives and friends with positions in the Church. Too often the needs of people were neglected. Churchmen would chase many positions simply for the wealth they provided. Priests were not supposed to have anything to do with women. But many lived with women and had children as well!

If the Catholic Church were to improve, reform had to come from the Pope himself. At first this did not happen. Instead, groups and societies organized themselves locally. They were dedicated to providing a good education for future priests and getting closer to the people. They wanted to show that the Church could look after the bodies and souls of people. The Ursuline nuns, for instance, worked with the poor, the sick and the young. They became well known for teaching girls.

The most effective organization was the **Society of Jesus**, set up by a Spanish nobleman, **Ignatius Loyola** (1491–1556). He soon attracted many followers and the Society gained the official backing of Pope Paul III in 1540. The members, known as **Jesuits**, pledged themselves to obey and work for the Pope. They concentrated on training priests and missionaries, who then spread the Catholic message to the people. Their main targets were in Europe, but they were also active overseas, even as far as Japan. **Francis Xavier** (1506–52) was one of their leading missionaries.

Ignatius Loyola before Pope Paul III, about 1540.

Source A

I came out from Portugal on the same ship as Father Francis. I often watched him at his charitable occupations and while he taught Christian doctrine. He used to beg alms from other passengers for the poor and sick persons. He took personal charge of those who were sick or prostrated by illness. From this work of mercy, and from his hearing of confessions, he allowed himself never a moment's respite, but cheerfully accomplished it all. Everybody held him for a saint, and that was my own fixed opinion.

A surgeon on the ship on which Francis Xavier sailed to the East, 1541.

Source B

I recognize the Holy Catholic and Apostolic Roman Church as the mother and mistress of all churches. And I vow and swear true obedience to the Roman Pontiff [Pope], the successor of blessed Peter, the chief of the Apostles and the representative of Jesus Christ.

The statement all priests had to make after the Council of Trent.

Source C

While Loyola's Jesuits were beginning the work of reform, Pope Paul III called the leaders of the Church together at the **Council of Trent**. He wanted to reunite the Christian world and reorganize the Church. He hoped that if the Christians of Europe were united, they could stand firm against the expansion of the Muslim Turks. Several meetings took place between 1545 and 1563. They all failed to persuade Protestants to return to the Catholic faith.

However, the Council of Trent gave Catholics a new confidence. It made clear the main features of their faith. Obedience to the Pope, the importance of Latin and the decoration of churches by paintings were all confirmed. But, rather than reunite Christianity, the council made clear the differences between Protestants and Catholics. Each form of the Christian religion was now in competition with the others.

The Council of Trent began the revival of the Catholic Church. The worst faults were gradually removed. With the help of the Jesuits, the Church reached out to the people.

Source D

The Council of Trent (1545–63). A painting by Titian.

Source E

Almost the last act of the Council of Trent had been to put forward a series of decrees on the nature of purgatory, relics, the worship of saints and images, and indulgences. It was an act of defiance. It was a forceful statement of all that the Protestants hated.

From Michael J. Walsh, 'The Council of Trent', 1974.

Questions

Section A

1 Was the Counter-Reformation started to face the challenge set by Protestants? Explain your answer carefully.

2 How did the Society of Jesus help to reform the Catholic Church?

3 How can Source A help to explain the success of the Jesuits?

4 In what way is Source B giving the same evidence as Source C?

5 How does the painter of Source D show that the Council of Trent was an important occasion?

Section B

6 What were the most important changes in the Catholic Church brought about by the Counter-Reformation?

7 Make a list of the ways in which the Catholic Church did **not** change, as shown by Sources B and E.

8 a Look carefully at the paragraph dealing with the faults of the Catholic Church. Discuss in pairs which faults were likely to take longer to change than others.

 b Suggest reasons why some faults in the Church took longer to change than others.

3.2 Persecution and Toleration

In the 16th and 17th centuries most Europeans believed that the **way** God was worshipped was very important. Worshipping God in the wrong way could cause someone to go to hell and not to heaven. Many Protestants, for instance, believed that the Pope was a servant of the Antichrist (the Devil). Some of them even believed that the Pope was the Devil himself. At the same time most people involved in politics believed that everyone in a country had to be of the same faith or there would always be revolts. This meant that **religious toleration** seemed wrong to most people. They believed that everyone should be forced to be of the correct faith. This would keep the country safe and save people from hell.

During the Reformation, the methods used to keep people practising religion in a uniform way became increasingly tough and violent. Treating people badly for their beliefs, or for simply being different, is called **persecution.**

Catholics were persecuted in Protestant areas and Protestants in Catholic areas. Many people were attacked and forced to leave their homes. Some were accused of heresy and burned at the stake.

This happened all over Europe, but nowhere more so than in Spain and the other lands controlled by the Spanish king, Philip II. It was the job of the **Inquisition** to force obedience to the Catholic Church. The Inquisition was a special kind of court. The job of this court was to find and punish those who disagreed with the Catholic Church and its leaders. People were expected to make a public statement of faith known as **auto-da-fé** in a ceremony. If they refused, they could be sentenced to death by burning.

In some places, however, toleration was practised. After long and violent wars over religion in France, Henry IV granted religious freedom to the Huguenots (Protestants).

Source A

> **Article 3** We ordain that the Catholic faith be restored in all those districts and places of this our Realm.
>
> **Article 6** And to leave no occasion for trouble among our subjects: We permit those of the so-called Reformed Religion to live and abide free from inquisition, molestation or compulsion.

Extracts from the Edict of Nantes, 1598, in which Henry IV of France gave religious freedom to the Huguenots (Protestants).

Special clothes worn by people condemned by the Inquisition. Those with drawings of flames on their clothes were allowed to live because they had repented. Those with flames and devils on their clothes were to be burned. From a 16th-century French print.

Source C

A 15th-century Spanish painting showing members of the Inquisition and the burning of condemned people.

Source D

If he refuses to be converted, he is sent to a large town to be burned on the pyre, perhaps alone, perhaps with others like him. Wearing a gown on which are pictures of devils pulling him into hell and tormenting him in a thousand ways, he is put to death in the most atrocious manner, and his picture is exhibited in the cathedrals to perpetuate his shame. But, for the martyrs, this death is glory, as indeed it is thus to suffer persecution and death for the true religion of Jesus Christ.

A Swiss traveller writing in 1599. He is describing the treatment of Protestants by the Inquisition.

Questions

Section A

1 Why did toleration seem a bad idea to many people?

2 What did the Inquisition do?

3 Source D tells us that many people were proud to die for their beliefs. Do you think that the methods of the Inquisition worked? Explain your answer.

Section B

4 Do Sources B, C and D support one another in any way?

5 a Is Source C realistic?
  b Do you think historians would find Source C useful?

6 a Do you think Source D was written by a Catholic or a Protestant?
  b Would definitely knowing the answer to part **a** change the way a historian would use Source D?

7 Which of these sources is most useful for showing the way 16th-century people felt about religion and toleration? Give reasons for your answer.

3.3 The Civil Wars in France

For nearly 30 years after 1562, France was torn apart by **civil war** between the Protestants and the Catholics. Because the two sides were divided by religion, the wars are sometimes called the **Wars of Religion**. However, there was also a struggle for power between different groups of nobles.

The French kings were weak at this time. They found it hard to keep the country together. Many classes were discontented. In some cities and provinces the authority of the French government was not recognized. There was a danger of France falling apart.

Many French people became Protestant. By 1562 the influence of Calvin was very strong. His supporters in France, the **Huguenots**, were well organized and claimed to have 2,000 churches all over France. They never amounted to more than 10 per cent of the population. However, they had powerful supporters among the French nobles. Their two most important leaders were **Condé** and **Coligny**.

The Huguenots were under constant threat of attack. Strict laws against heresy were introduced. The Inquisition searched for heretics. Coligny believed that the only way for the Huguenots to defend themselves was by organizing as a military force. First, he wanted freedom of worship from the French government. He hoped that eventually Protestants would rule France.

In 1559, the King of France was the young Charles IX. His mother, Catherine de Medici, wanted to restore the power of the Crown. She cared little for religion. In 1562 she offered the Huguenots the right to worship freely, hoping to get their support. But this enraged the Catholics. The Catholic **Duke of Guise** massacred the Huguenots at Vassy and then stormed into Paris and captured the king. Later, the Duke of Guise was killed and the king freed, but the wars dragged on. Occasional truces between the warring groups failed to last very long. No one side was much stronger than the other. With the involvement of foreign armies – the Catholics of Spain and the Protestants of the Netherlands – the wars continued.

These wars were particularly vicious and violent in a violent age. In 1572 the queen grew concerned at the amount of influence the Huguenot leader Coligny had over her son. She plotted to have Coligny assassinated. This led to the most famous and worst incident of the wars: the **St Bartholomew's Day massacre**.

Source A

It would be impossible to tell you what barbarous cruelties are committed by both sides. Where the Huguenot is master, he ruins the images and demolishes the sepulchres and tombs. On the other hand, the Catholic kills, murders and drowns all those whom he knows to be of that sect, until the rivers overflow with them.

A contemporary French writer commenting on the Wars of Religion.

Source B

A Frenchman and an Englishman who are of the same religion have more affection for one another than citizens of the same city, or slaves of the same land.

The French chancellor (a leading minister) commenting at the time on the religious differences in France.

Source C

While the usual title 'French Wars of Religion' is inadequate, the opposite tendency, to minimize the role of religion, is also wrong.

From A. G. Dickens, 'The Age of Humanism and Reformation', 1972

Source D

You must surrender to your enemies, or defeat them, or turn Catholic.

The advice given to Henry IV of France (reigned 1593–1614) by one of his ministers.

Source E

The St Bartholomew's Day massacre in Paris, 1572.

While Coligny and other Huguenots were in Paris for the wedding of the king's sister, they were attacked in their beds. The Paris mob supported the Catholics and celebrated. Soon they were out of control and butchered over 1,000 victims. It was a signal for attacks on Huguenots all over France. It is thought that more than 10,000 people were killed.

There was little chance of a lasting peace until someone who could gain the support of both Catholics and Protestants became king. This was achieved when the Protestant King of France **Henry IV** converted to the Catholic faith in 1593. Eventually he was able to give the Huguenots freedom of religion by the **Edict of Nantes** in 1598.

Questions

Section A

1 Draw a timeline to show the events in France between 1562 and 1598.

2 What were the main aims of Catherine de Medici and Henry IV?

Section B

3 Study Source E
  a How has the artist shown the St Bartholomew's Day massacre?
  b Do you think the artist was a Catholic or a Protestant?
  c Do historians need to know the answer to part **b** when using this source?

4 Historians call some sources **unwitting sources**. These are sources which were created as part of the actions and events in the past, not sources which were created to tell people what happened.
  a Are any of the sources in this unit unwitting sources?
  b What advantages might unwitting sources have for historians?

3.4 *The Dutch Revolt*

In 1559 the **Netherlands** was part of the Holy Roman Empire ruled by the Hapsburg family. Philip II of Spain inherited this Empire after the death of Charles V. At that time the Netherlands was made up of what is now Luxemburg, Belgium and the modern Netherlands. By the end of the 16th century, the northern part of the Netherlands had broken away from the Empire and had formed the independent state of the **United Provinces**. This unit explains how and why this happened.

The Dutch had begun to feel that they were a nation before Philip became king. Most were loyal Catholics, but, unlike Philip, they were prepared to tolerate a range of different beliefs. Close to the sea, the area around Antwerp had developed as a great trading and financial centre. With the Netherlands so far from the centre of power in Spain, it was difficult for Philip to rule anyway. However, he made a number of mistakes.

Charles V had been a Netherlander by upbringing. He had been able to keep control and still give the people a feeling of freedom. Philip did not understand or trust the Netherlanders. Instead of allowing the local nobles to have a say in the running of the government, he told his regent to keep them out of important decisions. They responded by trying to gain more power in their own areas.

Source A

An engraving made in about 1579 showing Calvinists attacking images in churches in the Netherlands.

Source B

King Philip II of Spain (reigned 1556–98) by an unknown artist, about 1580.

Source C

As to the Inquisition, my will is that it be enforced by the Inquisitors, as is required by all law human and divine. This lies very near my heart and I require you to carry out my orders. Let all prisoners be put to death, and suffer them no longer to escape through the neglect, weakness and bad faith of the judges. If any are too timid to execute the edicts, I will replace them by men who have more heart and zeal.

A letter written by Philip II of Spain in 1565 to his regent in the Netherlands.

Philip was a devout Catholic. In 1561 he tried to reorganize the Church in the Netherlands, giving **Granvelle**, his representative, the most powerful position in the Church. Philip felt that too much freedom had been allowed to 'heretics' in the past. He expected the Inquisition to wipe them out. The nobles, led by **William of Orange**, complained and forced Philip to dismiss Granvelle. However, the king had no intention of relaxing his control or allowing 'heresy' to go unpunished (Source C).

Calvinism had spread rapidly through the Netherlands. Faced with the threat of persecution, the Protestants talked of armed resistance. In 1565 harvest failure led to unemployment and hunger. In 1566 there were outbreaks of mob violence – especially attacks on churches and image breaking. Philip sent the **Duke of Alva** to crush the uprising in 1567. William of Orange became the leader of the Dutch opposition to their Spanish rulers. Philip put a price on his head.

The Duke of Alva and his troops used terror and violence in trying to put down the revolt. This succeeded only in turning people against Spain. Many Dutch people joined the Calvinist faith, especially in the provinces of the north. More wished to be free from Spain.

However, there were deep divisions among the people of the Netherlands. The southern part of the Netherlands had stayed more loyal to the Catholic Church. In 1579 the southern nobles formed the **Union of Arras**, and were prepared to work with Spain. The northern provinces replied with the **Union of Utrecht**. It was now a matter of how much of the Netherlands would gain its freedom.

The **Duke of Parma** was appointed Governor of the Netherlands by Philip in 1578. His task was to win back the north of the Netherlands for Spain. At first he did well. In 1583 William of Orange was assassinated as Philip had ordered. The Duke of Parma won back some key towns like Brussels and Antwerp. But William's son, **Maurice**, soon proved himself to be a great military leader as the new head of the rebels. He was able to win back some territory from the Spanish, and by 1593 there was a stalemate. The **United Provinces** declared itself an independent **republic,** though this was not accepted by Spain until 1648.

Source D

> I take it as an honour that I have been denounced by the Spanish King for leading your cause and that of freedom and independence. For this I am called traitor, heretic, foreigner, rebel, enemy of the human race. And I am to be killed like a wild beast, with a price offered to my assassins. I am no foreigner here, no rebel, no traitor.

An open letter from William of Orange to all the people of the Netherlands, 1568.

Source E

> I, with above 10,000 more, went into the churches to see what stir there was there. Coming into our Lady Church, it looked like a hell. There were above 1,000 torches burning, and such a noise, as if heaven and earth had gone down together, with falling of images and beating down of costly works; in such sort that a man could not well pass through the church.

An English traveller reporting from Antwerp in the Netherlands, 1566.

Questions

Section A

1 How can you tell from Sources A and E that Calvinists thought it was wrong to decorate churches with pictures and statues?

2 What evidence is there in Source C that Philip felt that Dutch Catholics had allowed the Calvinists too much freedom?

3 What sort of person do you think William of Orange was? Use Source D to help you explain your answer.

Section B

4 The Dutch Revolt had a number of **causes**. Study the following list carefully.
- The Dutch felt that they were members of a Dutch nation.
- The Dutch allowed freedom of belief.
- Philip kept Dutch nobles out of important decisions.
- Philip insisted on the burning of heretics by the Inquisition.
- Bad harvests led to unemployment and hunger.
- Calvinists attacked churches.

a Explain why **each** was a cause of the revolt.
b List the causes under the following headings: **religious, political, economic**.
c Explain how the causes of the revolt were linked to one another.
d Discuss in groups how important the religious causes of the revolt were. Write down the main points of your discussion.

4.1 Elizabeth I and Religion

Many problems faced the young **Queen Elizabeth I** when she came to the throne in November 1558. Many people had become Protestants during the reigns of Henry VIII and Edward VI. But her sister, Mary I, had made Catholicism the official religion in England. In her **religious settlement** Elizabeth tried to please both religious groups. In 1559 she asked Parliament to pass the **Act of Supremacy** and the **Act of Uniformity**. The first made Elizabeth the governor of the Church of England. The second said that the English Book of Common Prayer was to be used in all church services and that all English people were to attend church every Sunday. People who did not go were called **recusants** and were fined one shilling.

Many people were happy with these new arrangements. Strict Catholics, however, were upset that they could no longer say **mass** and that the Pope was not the head of the Church. Strict Protestants (or **Puritans**) were angry that Elizabeth had kept bishops to run the new **Anglican Church** and that clergymen were to be allowed to wear vestments. The Puritans believed that the Anglican Church should be purified of all things Catholic – even down to removing the candles on the altar. Elizabeth, in their opinion, had not gone far enough.

To begin with, the Catholics seemed to go along with the changes. Some attended church but took no notice of the service. Others just paid the fine. As long as they did not bother Elizabeth, she left them in peace. Two great foreign Catholic countries, France and Spain, could have tried to enforce the Catholic religion on England, but they did not interfere at first. The French Catholics were too busy fighting the Protestants in their own country. Philip II of Spain thought that Elizabeth would, in time, make England a Catholic country. He also had hopes of marrying Elizabeth and did not want a quarrel. But from 1569, things changed.

First, in 1569 a group of Catholics led by the **Earls of Northumberland** and **Cumberland** rose in rebellion against Elizabeth. They went into Durham Cathedral where they tore up the English Prayer Book and said mass. They demanded that England should become a Catholic country again. Elizabeth had to assert her power. Northumberland was captured and executed.

Second, the Counter-Reformation was underway in Europe. The Catholic Church was trying to reassert its power. In 1570, a new Pope came to office. He issued a **bull** (official order) which **excommunicated** (expelled) Elizabeth from the Catholic Church.

Source A

Elizabeth I wanted to keep her country united and avoid civil war.

From J. A. P. Jones, 'The Early Modern World 1450–1700', 1979.

Source B

John Stubbs, a Puritan, published a pamphlet in 1583 criticizing Elizabeth for saying she would marry a French prince. Stubbs is shown here having his right hand chopped off. As this was happening, Stubbs called out: 'God save the queen!'

The Pope also said that she was illegitimate and therefore not the lawful Queen of England. The proper queen was Mary Queen of Scots, a Catholic. The bull had the effect of encouraging a number of Catholics to plot against Elizabeth. The English government now saw every Catholic as a threat to Elizabeth's throne.

Meanwhile, in Europe, English Catholics were being trained as priests. They were then sent back to England as missionaries to strengthen the Catholic faith. The missionaries had to be careful not to get caught. They hid in secret places (called **priest-holes**) in the houses of rich Catholics. In 1581 a Catholic missionary, **Edmund Campion**, was captured. He was tortured, found guilty of plotting to overthrow Elizabeth and hanged. Campion denied the charges and said he was loyal to Elizabeth. There followed a clamp-down on the Catholics; the fine for not attending church was raised to £20.

The Puritans were another problem for Elizabeth. They wanted bishops abolished and worship to be as simple as possible. They believed in plain churches and long sermons. They were totally against entertainment such as theatre-going. There were many Puritans in the House of Commons.

It had always been the monarch's right to decide what should be discussed by Parliament. Elizabeth banned any talk about religion or the question of whether she should get married. The Puritans, however, now started to demand the right to have freedom of speech by discussing any issue that they wanted. This was a direct challenge to the authority of the queen, who looked upon herself as the head of the government.

Source C

A contempary print showing two Catholic missionary priests of the period, Edmund Campion and Robert Parsons.

Source D

The Catholics discovered that if they did not make plots they had only the fines to fear.

From M. M. Reese, 'Tudors and Stuarts', 1971.

Questions

Section A

1 a Who do you think published Source C and why?

  b Does this source prove that Campion plotted to overthrow Elizabeth? Explain your answer.

2 Elizabeth thought that Puritans were a nuisance. Why then did Stubbs call out 'God save the queen'? Give reasons for your answer.

3 Judging by Source B, do you think the Elizabethans were cruel people? Explain your answer.

Section B

4 Look back at Units 2.3–2.5.
  a What changes were made in religion by:
  ● Henry VIII
  ● Edward VI
  ● Mary I?

  b How did Elizabeth change religion when she came to the throne in 1558?

  c Why did Elizabeth make such changes?

5 Do you think people at the time would have looked on Elizabeth's religious settlement as a change for the better? Give reasons for your answer.

6 Did the events of 1570 bring about any changes in England? Explain your answer.

7 'The Puritans wanted both political and religious changes.' Do you agree with this statement? Give reasons for your answer.

4.2 Images of Elizabeth I

Many people today are fascinated by the royal family. Queen Elizabeth II is seen by millions of people each year, either in person, on television or in the newspapers. In the 16th century, people had a similar interest in **Queen Elizabeth I**. But, unlike today, few people were able to see her in real life. Ordinary people were unable to visit London. The only chance they got to see the queen was when she went on a **royal progress** (tour). This took place in the summer, when the queen and her courtiers left London. They would stay in large country houses at the invitation of wealthy noblemen.

The only other way of seeing what Queen Elizabeth looked like was by looking at a **portrait**. At first, Elizabeth was not keen on having her portrait painted. She had caught smallpox in 1562 and this usually left huge pit-marks on a person's face. Her ministers, however, told her that it was important for the people to see her. Owning a portrait of the monarch was a way of showing loyalty; in fact, from 1570 onwards there was a big demand for portraits of the queen.

Elizabeth, however, posed only for a few selected painters. She insisted that any portrait of her should be based on an 'approved' pattern, so that her face and costume were always shown in a certain way. Many paintings, medals and woodcuts portraying Elizabeth were produced during her reign. It should therefore be easy to describe exactly what she looked like – or should it?

Source A

Elizabeth I in her coronation robes. This portrait became the approved pattern for official paintings of the queen.

Source B

A portrait of Elizabeth painted in 1588.

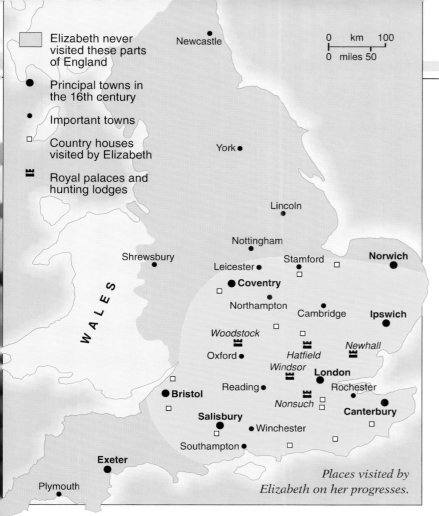

Elizabeth never visited these parts of England

● Principal towns in the 16th century

• Important towns

□ Country houses visited by Elizabeth

♔ Royal palaces and hunting lodges

0 km 100
0 miles 50

Newcastle

York ●

Lincoln ●

Nottingham ●

Shrewsbury ●

Leicester ●

Stamford □ □

Norwich ●

Coventry ●
□

Northampton ●

Cambridge ●

Ipswich ●

Woodstock □
♔

Newhall ♔

Oxford ●

Hatfield ♔

Windsor ♔

London ●

Reading ●

Rochester ●

□

□

Nonsuch ♔ □

Canterbury ●

● **Bristol**

Salisbury ●

Winchester ●

□ □

Southampton ● □

Exeter

Plymouth

W A L E S

Places visited by Elizabeth on her progresses.

Questions

Section A

1 Why might Queen Elizabeth have gone on royal progresses?

2 What do you notice about the parts of England that Elizabeth visited? Can you explain this?

Section B

3 Use the sources provided in this unit to describe the appearance of Elizabeth I in your own words.

4 Which was more useful to you in answering question **3**: the paintings or the written description? Give reasons for your answer.

5 a What do you think Elizabeth wanted Source A to show?
  b What do you think Elizabeth wanted Source B to show?
  c What do you think Elizabeth wanted Source D to show?

6 How far would you trust Sources A, B and D as evidence of what Elizabeth I looked like? Explain your answer.

7 'Because we have a large number of portraits of Elizabeth I, it is easy to say exactly what she looked like.' Do you agree or disagree with this statement? Give reasons for your answer.

8 'Sources which are unreliable are useless to historians.' Judging by the sources in this unit, do you agree or disagree with this statement? Give reasons for your. answer.

Source C

Next came the queen, very majestic. Her face oblong, fair but wrinkled; her eyes small, yet black and pleasant; her nose a little hooked, her lips narrow, her teeth black; her hair was of auburn colour, but false. Her hands were slender, her fingers rather long, and her height neither tall nor low.

From Paul Hentzner, 'Travels in England in the Reign of Queen Elizabeth', 1889, describing a procession in 1598.

Source D

Elizabeth in a procession at Blackfriars in 1600.

4.3 Wales and Ireland

Wales

In 1536 and 1543 Henry VIII passed two **Acts of Union** which united England with **Wales**. From this time onwards Wales had the same laws as England and sent MPs to represent Wales in Parliament. English became the language used in Welsh courts of law and new counties were formed in the areas which had previously been controlled by the marcher lords. The fact that Henry VII had been Welsh meant that the Tudor monarchs were accepted by the people of Wales.

Ireland

Relations with Ireland were more troubled. The English had claimed **Ireland** as their own since 1155. Henry VIII gave himself the title 'King of Ireland' and tried to get the Irish to turn away from the Pope and become Protestants. However, most Irish people saw their clan chief as their real leader and they were determined to remain Catholics. When Elizabeth I's **religious settlement** confirmed England as a Protestant country, the problem became worse. There was now a strong possibility that Ireland could be used as a base by England's Catholic enemies (such as Spain). They could then invade England more easily.

Elizabeth decided to **colonize** Ireland. This involved taking land away from the Irish and giving it to English Protestant settlers. Not surprisingly, the Irish objected to such treatment and there were several rebellions against the English. The most serious one took place between 1595 and 1603. It was led by **Hugh O'Neill (Earl of Tyrone)** and **Hugh O'Donnell**.

At first the Irish beat the English forces, and the rising spread from the province of Ulster to the rest of Ireland. In April 1599 the **Earl of Essex** arrived with a large English army. But he was not very successful. He made a truce with Tyrone – against the wishes of Elizabeth – and then returned to England. Worse still, in 1601 a Spanish army arrived at **Kinsale** to help the Irish. But the English increased their efforts. **Lord Mountjoy** surrounded Kinsale with English troops. Gradually they got the upper hand. By early 1603 the Irish surrendered. The whole of Ireland was now under the control of the English.

Source A

The desperate Irish found a real leader in Hugh O'Neill, Earl of Tyrone. He so rattled the English that the dashing Earl of Essex had to be sent out in 1599. Essex made a sad mess of the campaign against Tyrone and could do no more than obtain a truce. The testy old queen was furious. Essex, brave and foolish, rushed home to confront his enemies at court who were poisoning the queen's mind against him. Dusty and bedraggled from the journey, he burst into the royal apartments but was coldly dismissed for his impertinence. Essex then behaved like a naughty child, gathering desperate men about him and indulging in wild plans to overthrow the council. His arrest for treason followed, for, though Elizabeth had doted on the wilful, gifted youth, she could not forgive a rebellious nobleman.

From R. J. Unstead, 'Crown and Parliament 1485–1688', 1962.

Source B

Contrary to orders forbidding his return, Essex left Ireland in a rage. On 28 September 1599 he reached Nonsuch Palace. He strode upstairs to the private apartments, and burst into the sovereign's chamber. Elizabeth, just out of bed, had not begun her elaborate toilet. Essex saw her as no man before: without her wig and her rouge, her ruff and her mass of jewels. Stunned by his arrival, she let him kiss her hand, and then he left to change his clothes.

From Neville Williams, 'Elizabeth I', 1972.

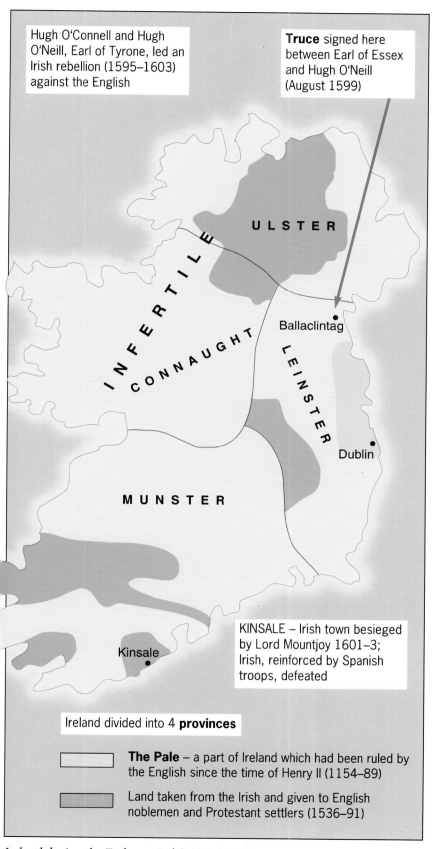

Hugh O'Connell and Hugh O'Neill, Earl of Tyrone, led an Irish rebellion (1595–1603) against the English

Truce signed here between Earl of Essex and Hugh O'Neill (August 1599)

ULSTER

INFERTILE

CONNAUGHT

LEINSTER

Ballaclintag

Dublin

MUNSTER

Kinsale

KINSALE – Irish town besieged by Lord Mountjoy 1601–3; Irish, reinforced by Spanish troops, defeated

Ireland divided into 4 **provinces**

The Pale – a part of Ireland which had been ruled by the English since the time of Henry II (1154–89)

Land taken from the Irish and given to English noblemen and Protestant settlers (1536–91)

Ireland during the Tudor period (1485–1603).

Source C

Mountjoy found, hidden behind boggy land, west of Philipstown, a prosperous territory. 'It is incredible,' he said, 'in so barbarous a country how well the ground was manured, how orderly the fields were fenced, their towns inhabited and paths so well beaten.' His troops, by burning the houses and cutting the corn with their swords, brought savagery with them.

From 'A New History of Ireland', 1976, written by G. Hoyes-McCoy, an Irish historian.

Questions

Section A

1 How did the Tudors unite England and Wales?

2 What part did the following people play in the story of Ireland in the 16th century:
- Henry VIII
- the Earl of Tyrone
- the Earl of Essex
- the Spanish
- Lord Mountjoy?

Section B

3 Quote two **facts** and two **points of view** in Source A. Explain your answer.

4 a Using only the **map** in this unit, write a paragraph describing events in Ireland in the Tudor period.

b Would your account have differed if you had been allowed to use any of the other sources? Explain your answer.

c Why do historians use as many sources as possible when trying to find out about past events?

5 a Sources A and B give different interpretations of what happened when Essex returned from Ireland. Explain **how** they differ.

b Why do you think they differ?

6 Some writers give a stereotyped picture of Ireland in the 16th century, leading us to believe it was a place of boggy swamps. How does Source C differ? Explain why this might be so.

4.4 Rich and Poor

Sometime I, like a cripple,
Upon the ground lie crawling.
For money I beg, as wanting a leg,
To bear my corpse from falling.

From 'The Cunning Northern Beggar', a popular song of the period.

In 1586 **William Harrison** wrote a book called ***Descriptions of England***. He said there were five different groups of people in England. Harrison called the richest people the **greater gentlemen**. They owned large houses and usually filled the top positions in the government. Many of them regularly attended Queen Elizabeth's court. The **lesser gentlemen** were important in local affairs, serving as Justices of the Peace (magistrates). The **citizens** were freemen living in the towns. This group also included a growing number of merchants who benefited from the opening up of new trade routes. The **yeomen** were farmers who owned or rented some land. They, too, prospered during Elizabeth's reign. The largest of Harrison's groups, the **day labourers**, included craftspeople, shopkeepers and farmworkers. These people were not rich but they managed to make a living.

During Elizabeth's reign, **poverty** became a very serious problem. The elderly and sick who were unable to work were known as the '**impotent poor**'. These people depended on charity or begging to keep alive. In addition, there were the '**sturdy beggars**'. These were able-bodied people who were out of work and so turned to begging. The number of people begging rose noticeably at this time.

Source A

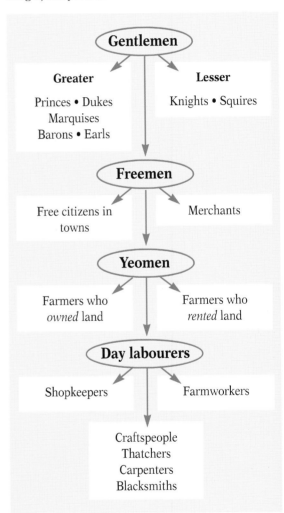

Social groupings in Elizabethan England.

Vagrants being punished, late 1500s.

Many sturdy beggars became **vagrants**, moving from town to town in search of a job. A large number headed for London. So many went that the authorities had to provide hospitals for the sick and set up a 'bridewell' (a 'house of correction' or prison) where the able-bodied poor were made to work. It was generally thought that all sturdy beggars were work-shy, lazy criminals; they were also called 'the idle poor'. The Puritans preached that unemployed people were sinners against God and should be punished.

The **punishments** for vagrancy were harsh. When caught, vagrants could be whipped and burned through the right ear. If they were caught again they could even be hanged. The government did not seem to realize that many people wanted to work but found it impossible to get a job (see diagram).

By the end of Elizabeth's reign, however, **attitudes towards the poor** began to change. In Ipswich, the impotent poor were allowed to beg. They were given badges to show they were genuinely ill or disabled. The government realized that not all sturdy beggars were rogues and criminals; some actually wanted to work but, because of the lack of jobs, were unable to find any.

An **Act of 1601** said that each parish in England had to look after its own poor. An **overseer** was to be appointed to collect a **poor rate** to pay for looking after the poor. The impotent poor would be given help and the able-bodied poor given work to do in a workhouse. The goods they made would be sold and they would get paid. Vagrants who wandered away from their own parish were to be whipped and sent back home.

Source C

Types of beggars, late 1500s.

Questions

Section A

1 Design and draw your own diagram to show the different groups in Elizabethan society.

2 Was poverty a **new** problem in Elizabethan times? Give reasons for your answer.

3 What sorts of different beggars are shown in Source C? How can you tell?

Section B

4 Study Source A. How does this treatment of the poor differ from the way that poor people are treated today?

5 If the punishments for vagrants were so harsh, why did the numbers increase during Elizabeth's reign?

6 What would the people shown watching in Source A have thought about the treatment of the vagrants? Explain your answer.

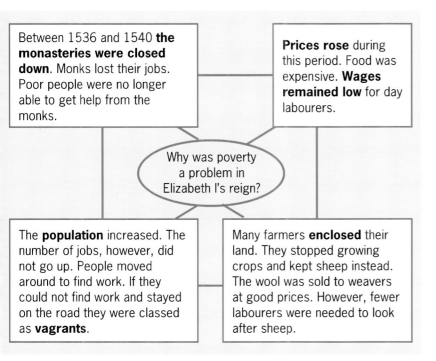

Between 1536 and 1540 **the monasteries were closed down**. Monks lost their jobs. Poor people were no longer able to get help from the monks.

Prices rose during this period. Food was expensive. **Wages remained low** for day labourers.

Why was poverty a problem in Elizabeth I's reign?

The **population** increased. The number of jobs, however, did not go up. People moved around to find work. If they could not find work and stayed on the road they were classed as **vagrants**.

Many farmers **enclosed** their land. They stopped growing crops and kept sheep instead. The wool was sold to weavers at good prices. However, fewer labourers were needed to look after sheep.

Causes of poverty in Elizabethan England.

4.5 Mary Queen of Scots

Mary was born in 1542. She was the daughter of James V of Scotland and Mary of Guise. Her father died when she was just a few days old. Mary was crowned **Queen of Scotland**; but, because she was too young to rule, her mother carried out the duties of the monarch.

In 1548 Mary was sent to be brought up and educated in France. She enjoyed life at the French court, and when she was 15 years old she married Prince Francis, the eldest son of the French king. In 1559 her husband became king but, tragically for Mary, he died in 1560.

Source A

The Queen of Scots sat on a stool, in her hand a crucifix. She began with tears in her eyes to pray loudly in Latin. When she had finished she was stripped of her outer garments and blindfolded. She knelt down upon the cushion, without any sign of fear of death, and, groping for the block, she laid down her head. Then she cried out: 'Into your hands, O Lord!' three or four times. She endured two strokes of the executioner's axe, and made a very small noise, and so the executioner cut off her head, except for a small piece of gristle. Then he lifted up her head and shouted: 'God save the queen!'

An eyewitness account of the execution of Mary Queen of Scots.

Source B

An anonymous painting of the execution of Mary Queen of Scots in 1587.

Mary returned to Scotland in 1561. She found that her native country had become Protestant in religion. Mary had to accept this but she continued to worship as a Catholic. In 1565 she married **Henry Stuart**, **Lord Darnley**. It was not a happy marriage, and Mary grew close to her Italian secretary, **David Rizzio**. Darnley became jealous; on 9 March 1566 he and a group of friends murdered Rizzio at **Holyrood Palace**. On 19 June 1566 Mary gave birth to a son, James, who later became king of both Scotland and England.

Mary became friendly with **James Hepburn, Earl of Bothwell**. At about this time, Darnley fell ill with smallpox. Mary had him brought to Kirk o'Field, a large house in Edinburgh. She nursed him daily. On 9 February 1567 Mary left early to attend a wedding. That night the house was blown up. However, when Darnley's body was discovered in the garden, it was found that he had been strangled.

Bothwell was put on trial, accused of murdering Darnley. He was found not guilty. Some time afterwards the **casket letters** were discovered. Elizabeth's government said they had been written by Mary to Bothwell. In the letters it said that Mary wanted Darnley murdered. Mary argued that the letters were forgeries. Three months after Darnley's death, she married Bothwell.

The Scots rebelled against Mary. She was imprisoned in Lochleven Castle and in July 1567 was forced to **abdicate** (give up the throne). In May 1568 Mary escaped and fled to England. She was hopeful of getting help from her cousin, Elizabeth I. Mary's presence in England, however, gave Elizabeth a serious problem. What should she do with Mary? At first, Mary was held a prisoner in Carlisle.

In 1569 the **Northern Rebellion** took place. A group of Catholics planned to overthrow Elizabeth, but were discovered. Then, in 1570 the Pope excommunicated Elizabeth, officially expelling her from the Catholic Church. He also said that she was illegitimate and should not be Queen of England. Many Catholics believed that Mary was the rightful Queen of England. As long as Mary was in England, however, she would be a threat to Elizabeth's throne. Mary became the focus of plots to overthrow Elizabeth.

In 1571 a plot headed by **Robert Ridolfi** and the **Duke of Norfolk** was discovered. The plan was for a Spanish army to invade England and put Mary on the throne. The plot failed. Then, in 1586 **Francis Walsingham**, head of the Secret Service, uncovered the **Babington Plot**. Mary was found to be exchanging letters with a young Catholic called Anthony Babington. The letters were smuggled out of prison in beer barrels but were intercepted and decoded by Walsingham. The contents of the letters showed that Babington and his friends were plotting to release Mary and overthrow Elizabeth.

Elizabeth now came under strong pressure from her ministers to execute Mary. In October 1586 Mary was found guilty of treason. Very reluctantly, Elizabeth signed the death warrant. On 8 February 1587 Mary was beheaded in the great hall of **Fotheringhay Castle**.

Questions

Section A

1 Draw a **timeline** showing the main events of Mary's life.

2 What does Source A suggest about Mary's personality?

3 a Describe, in detail, the scene shown in Source B.
  b A number of people watched Mary's execution. Were they being cruel? Explain your answer.

4 Do you think the author of Source A was the same person who drew Source B? Explain your answer.

Section B

5 In 1568 Elizabeth could have sent Mary back to Scotland or even to France. Why do you think she kept her a prisoner in England instead?

6 Were the following events **causes** of Mary's execution:
  • Mary's marriage to Francis in 1557
  • the murder of Darnley
  • the excommunication of Elizabeth in 1570
  • Catholic plots against Elizabeth?
  Explain your answer in each case.

7 Which of the causes do you think was the most important?

8 Show in a diagram how the causes of Mary's execution are linked.

9 Was the execution of Mary inevitable (bound to have happened)? Explain your answer.

4.6 The Spanish Armada, 1588

A great deal has been written about the defeat of the **Spanish Armada**. In English textbooks the story is often told in a **one-sided** way. It is said that the English were far better at everything than the Spanish and this was the main reason why the Armada was beaten. The Elizabethans said this themselves so that national honour was kept up. This same story was passed down through time and grew into a **myth** (a fictitious story).

In recent years, however, books have been written which try to tell a more **objective** or **balanced** story. New evidence is being found all the time which changes historians' views about the Armada. For example, archaeological divers have recovered objects from the wrecks of the Spanish ships, and some historians have used Spanish accounts of the Armada. So historians are constantly making new interpretations about what happened in the summer of 1588.

Source A

The Spanish plan misfired for a number of reasons. The English were better sailors. Their ships were slightly smaller, could sail faster and had heavier firepower. The English also had better leaders. Lord Howard of Effingham and Sir Francis Drake were excellent commanders. The Spanish leader was the Duke of Medina Sidonia. He was seasick as soon as his flagship put out to sea. He was no match for his English rivals.

From Stephen White-Thomson, 'Elizabeth I and Tudor England', 1984.

Source B

The seamanship, discipline and fighting spirit of the Spaniards were superb. Keeping a tight formation, they moved slowly up the Channel for nine days, while the English fired their guns to no great purpose. The defeat of the Spanish Armada was not the fault of the Duke of Medina Sidonia, whose courage and leadership could hardly have been bettered.

From John Lynch, 'Spain under the Hapsburgs, 1516–1598', 1964.

Philip's plan – to invade England, the Armada aimed to sail to the Spanish Netherlands. Here it would collect soldiers under the Duke of Parma, cross to England, sail up the River Thames and conquer England. The plan almost succeeded but few books mention this. If the Spanish had landed in England they would have met with little resistance.

1 Armada left Lisbon, 20 May.

2 Armada put into Corunna to take in supplies, 9 June–12 July. Delayed by storms.

3 Armada sighted off the Lizard, 19 July.

4 Armada sailed up the English Channel in a crescent formation. English chased, 19–27 July.

5 Armada anchored off Calais, English sent in fire-ships. Armada cut their anchors, 28 July.

6 Battle of Gravelines, 29–30 July.

7 SW gale blew Armada northwards. Spanish attempted to return to Spain via north of Scotland. English chased until 2 August.

8 Armada reached Spain in September. Many ships (possibly 44) were wrecked off Scotland and Ireland.

Spanish commanded by the Duke of Medina Sidonia

English commanded by Lord Howard of Effingham

The route of the Armada.

Source C

A modern artist's interpretation of what happened when English fire-ships were floated towards the Armada. Taken from R.R. Selman, 'The Elizabethan Seaman', 1977.

Source D

There was not a single shot hole in a single English hull. A possible explanation has been offered by divers working on the Armada's wrecks. They have brought up guns and gunshot of every size. Most of the iron shot was very badly made and brittle. It also seems likely that the Spaniards damaged their own ships by firing guns that burst.

From David Howarth, 'The Voyage of the Armada: The Spanish Story', 1981.

Why the Armada sailed

Relations between Spain and England started to worsen in about 1569. Philip of Spain realized then that Elizabeth was not going to change her mind about England being a Protestant country.

Francis Drake and other English 'sea-dogs' attacked Spanish galleons as they returned from South America loaded with treasure.

In 1585 Elizabeth sent soldiers to help the Dutch Protestants fight against the Spanish. The Netherlands was occupied by Spain at this time. Philip was annoyed by this interference.

Philip began to make plans to invade England. In 1587 the execution of Mary, Queen of Scots, made him even more determined to invade England and make it a Catholic country.

Source E

Cannon balls found on board the wrecked 16th-century Spanish ship 'Santa Maria de la Rosa'.

Source F

One theory said that by the time the action off Gravelines was fought, the Spanish had used all their ammunition. This was not so. They simply did not fire their guns.

From Martin and Parker, 'The Spanish Armada', 1988, explaining why the English ships were not badly damaged.

Questions

Section A

1 Give one **long-term cause** and one **short-term cause** of the Armada sailing.

2 a What was the Spanish plan?
  b What happened after the Battle of Gravelines?

Section B

4 a Sources D and F agree that the English ships were not badly damaged. Do they give the same explanation?
  b Does Source E support the explanation given in Source D or Source F? Explain your answer.

5 Study Source A. Did things really happen like this? Give reasons for your answer.

6 Source C shows a modern interpretation of what happened when English fire-ships were floated into the Spanish fleet. How accurate do you think it is?

7 Sources D and F are interpretations based on archaeological findings. How accurate are they? Explain your answer.

8 Why do you think interpretations of the defeat of the Armada vary so much?

5.1 James I

In 1603 **Elizabeth I** was an old, sick and lonely woman. The men who had been her chief advisers were dead. She had refused to say who should rule England next. The obvious choice was **James VI of Scotland**, but other candidates were possible.

During March, Elizabeth's health got worse. She refused to go to bed. She would not eat and also refused to be treated by her doctors. One courtier, **Sir Robert Carey**, planned carefully what to do when she died. He arranged for a string of fast horses to be waiting between Richmond Palace, where Elizabeth was dying, and Edinburgh, where James VI was waiting for news. He hoped that if he were the first to tell James, he would be well rewarded.

On the night of 23–24 March, Carey waited in the gatehouse of the palace for a signal that Elizabeth had died. It came between 2 and 3 a.m. Carey began his ride. He arrived in Edinburgh late on 26 March and was the first to tell James of Elizabeth's death. Meanwhile, on 24 March, the Privy Council had proclaimed James King James I of England.

James was 37 years old. He had been a success in Scotland. He came to England with strong ideas on the powers that kings should have, but very little money. Scotland was poor compared to England.

As he came to London in 1603 James was welcomed by crowds in every town. But some things happened on his journey which were warnings for the rest of his reign. He never seemed to have enough money, and he had to send to the Privy Council in London for money and jewels for his journey. Also, James did not always understand the customs of his new country. When a pickpocket was caught in the crowd in Newark, James ordered that he should be hanged at once. After the pickpocket had been hanged, James's councillors quietly explained that in England the king did not have the power to have anyone put to death without trial.

In 1605 James I was persuaded by his ministers to clamp down on the Catholics. **Parliament** was due to meet on 5 November. **Lord Mounteagle**, a Catholic, was given a letter which warned him not to go. Mounteagle gave the letter to James and his ministers, who ordered a search to be made of the cellars under Parliament.

The searchers discovered a cellar full of gunpowder under the House of Lords. The House of Lords was where the king, the lords and most of the members of the House of Commons would be for the opening of Parliament. Also found in the cellar was a man who said his name was Johnson. Later he admitted he was **Guy Fawkes**.

Source A

The king's kindness has ended in this, Cecil told me. Catholic priests go openly about the country, saying mass, and this gives great offence to others. Nothing can be done. The laws must be obeyed. We cannot hope for good government while we have a large number of people who obey foreign rulers, as Catholics do. The priests preach that the Catholics must do everything to help their religion – even if it means killing the king.

An ambassador from a Catholic country, writing home, reporting the views of Robert Cecil about Catholics. Cecil (1563–1612) was James I's chief minister, responsible for security.

Source B

It has pleased almighty God to discover the most cruel and detestable plot. The plot was to kill the King, Queen, Prince, Council, Clergy, Judges and the principal gentlemen by secretly putting a great quantity of gunpowder into a cellar under Parliament, and so to have blown all up at a clap. God, out of his mercy and just revenge, allowed it to be discovered.

The main plotter is one Johnson, a Yorkshire man and servant to Thomas Percy. This Percy had, about a year and a half ago, hired a house by Parliament, from which he had access to the cellar to store his wood and coal. He is a Catholic, and so is his man Johnson. Into this cellar Johnson had carried a great quantity of powder, all of which he had cunningly covered with firewood. On Tuesday at midnight, as he was busy to prepare his things for explosion, he was caught in the place itself. There was found some fine powder, to make a fuse. He would have saved himself from the blow by some half an hour.

Robert Cecil writing to the English Ambassador in Brussels, 9 November 1605.

Source C

An early 17th-century print of the executions of the gunpowder plotters.

Source D

He said he did not intend to set fire to the fuse until the King came into the House, and then he intended to do it so the gunpowder might more surely blow up a quarter of an hour later.

From Guy Fawkes's confession, made after torture on 16 November 1605.

Source E

The lantern Guy Fawkes was carrying when he was arrested.

Questions

Section A

1 **a** Describe Sir Robert Carey's plan.
   b The Privy Council tried to stop Carey. Why might they have done this?

2 What two things happened on James I's journey south which were 'warnings for the rest of his reign'?

Section B

3 Why did Robert Cecil dislike the Catholics? Give reasons for your answer.

4 **a** Why did Cecil think that Percy was involved in the plot?
   b Why did Cecil think that Johnson was involved in the plot?

5 Is Source E of any use to historians studying the Gunpowder Plot?

6 Does Guy Fawkes's confession (Source D) **confirm** Cecil's story (Source B)? Explain your answer.

7 'Most people in England were glad that the Gunpowder Plot failed. And they came to hate the Catholics more because of it.'
   Does Source C support this view? Give reasons for your answer.

8 Is there enough evidence in this Unit to say who was responsible for the Gunpowder Plot? Explain your answer.

5.2 With and Without Parliament, 1603–40

James's problems

James held a conference about reforming the Church of England at Hampton Court in 1604. As well as the **Puritans**, who thought the Church was not Protestant enough, the people who were happy with the Church of England were there. The biggest disagreement was about the **bishops**. The Puritans wanted a Church without bishops. They thought the Church should be run by committees of ordinary church-goers. The bishops and their supporters wanted a Church run from the top. James agreed with the bishops. There was very little change in the Church of England. The most important thing to come out of the conference was probably the decision to make a new translation of the Bible.

The Puritans were still not happy with the Church of England. Most continued to go to the church services, but often complained about what went on. Some set up their own churches. They had to do this secretly because it was against the law.

Money was a big problem for James. He was expected to run the country on customs duties and the profits from the royal lands. He was only expected to need taxes when there was a war. In fact it cost more than this to run the country, even in a quiet year. But Parliament was not convinced – it thought the problem was caused by James giving away too much money to his favourites. In 1610 Parliament rejected a reform of the king's finances. James also failed to get the taxes he wanted from Parliament in 1614 and 1622.

James's problems with **foreign affairs** were tied up with religion and money. Europe was divided into Protestant and Catholic countries. The Catholic countries were more powerful. There was a danger that Protestantism would be destroyed. Many people in England believed that James should help the Protestants. They felt this particularly after 1618, when the **Thirty Years War**, a general war between Protestants and Catholics in Europe, broke out.

All these problems made things in Parliament worse. There were men in the two Houses who were Puritans; others thought James wasted money; and others thought England should fight in the Thirty Years War. Some people thought all three things. Successive parliaments complained about what was going on. They accused the king's favourites of dishonesty. They refused to grant him taxes.

Calling a Parliament

When Parliament meets, it is said to be **sitting**. Now it sits all the time, except during holidays and elections. In the 17th century, the monarch decided when to have one. When he or she wanted one, they **summoned** Parliament. Parliament had (and has) two parts, called Houses. The members of the **House of Lords** each get their own invitation. There are no elections; if you were (and are) a lord, you were (and are) always a member. Members of the **House of Commons** were (and are) elected.

Elections

There were two ways of becoming a **Member of Parliament** (MP) in the 17th century. Each county chose two MPs. The election was held on one day and in one place. The only people who could vote were men who owned land worth more than £2. The sheriff would read out the names of the candidates, and people shouted for the MPs they wanted. The sheriff decided who was given the loudest shout, and they were elected. If he wasn't sure, he got the supporters of each man to stand together in groups. He then decided which were the biggest groups. To count how many people wanted to vote for each man was very unusual.

The rest of the MPs were chosen by the **boroughs.** These were towns granted the right to send two MPs to Parliament by the king. Boroughs had all sorts of different ways of choosing MPs. In most, just the borough council could vote. In others, men who lived in certain houses (usually the houses of the rich) could vote. In one or two boroughs, all adult men could vote.

What Parliament did

The king needed Parliament to agree to all **taxes**. New laws could only be made if Parliament agreed to them. Kings and their ministers usually worked hard to get Parliament to do the things they wanted. Parliament also looked into **complaints** about the way the country was governed. Sometimes it asked the king to change things. This was called the **consideration of grievances.**

Source A

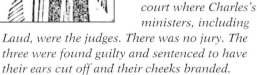

A cartoon of the period, showing Laud, Bastwick, Burton and Prynne. Bastwick, Burton and Prynne criticized Laud's changes in the Church. Arrested in 1637, they were tried in the Star Chamber. This was a special court where Charles's ministers, including Laud, were the judges. There was no jury. The three were found guilty and sentenced to have their ears cut off and their cheeks branded.

Later, things got even worse. There was a plan to marry James's son, Prince Charles, who would be the next king, to a Spanish princess. Spain had been England's enemy during Elizabeth's reign. Spain was also the leading Catholic power. Many people in Parliament objected to the plan.

Charles's problems

Charles I quarrelled with his first Parliament (1625) over taxes and his relations with Spain. Parliament decided to grant Charles the customs duties for one year only. These taxes were usually granted to a new king for life. Charles also quarrelled with his second Parliament (1626–7) over his favourite, the **Duke of Buckingham**. Many MPs thought that Buckingham had too much power. They were also worried that much of the king's money was given to favourites, rather than being used for the good of the country.

The worst quarrel of all was with the Parliament of 1628–9. Buckingham was dead, but Parliament was still not happy with the king's government. It criticized Charles for having Catholics at his court, for raising taxes without its permission, for changes in the Church of England and for his foreign policy. Finally Parliament complained about Charles trying to interfere with its work. Charles dismissed it and tried to govern without one.

The next eleven years, when there was no Parliament, are sometimes called the **Eleven Years Tyranny**. Charles had to get more money. He did this by bending the law. One tax he used was **Ship Money**. This was supposed to be for the navy. In the past, only towns near the coast had paid this tax. Charles made the whole country pay. Many people objected. They thought it was wrong for Charles to raise money without Parliament agreeing.

One of Charles's chief ministers was **William Laud, Archbishop of Canterbury**. Laud was changing the Church of England. He was making it more like the Catholic Church, and even less like the Church the Puritans wanted.

Questions

Section A

1 Draw a **timeline** from 1603 to 1640. Mark on the events mentioned in the text.

2 Look at Source A.
   a Which man is Laud?
   b Who do you think the two men standing behind the table with muskets are supposed to be?
   c What is being eaten?
   d Do you think the artist supported Laud?

Section B

3 Compare Parliament in the 17th century and Parliament today. Which things have changed and which have stayed the same? Use these headings:
   ● calling Parliament
   ● elections
   ● what Parliament does.

4 This unit describes a lot of changes that happened between 1603 and 1640.
   a List the changes under the following headings:
      ● religion
      ● finance
      ● foreign affairs
      ● Parliament.
   b Which do you think caused more trouble for James and Charles, the things that changed or the things that **didn't** change? Explain your answer.

5.3 Scotland and Ireland

The Arch-Prelate of S.t Andrewes in Scotland reading the new Service-booke in his pontificalibus assaulted by men & Women, with Cricketts stooles Stickes and Stones.

A 17th-century print about events in Scotland. 'Arch-prelate' is another way of saying 'archbishop'.

Scotland

Charles I was King of **Scotland** as well as of England. But the two countries were separate in other ways. Scotland had its own Parliament, its own laws and its own Church.

The Church in Scotland was a very strict Protestant one, called **Presbyterian**. Charles I wanted to make it less strict, like the Church of England. In July 1637 he ordered that all church services should be from a new prayer book, written by his English archbishop, William Laud. Most Scots wanted to keep their Presbyterian Church. There was a riot in Saint Giles Cathedral, Edinburgh, when the new prayer book was first used.

After the riot, a group called the **Covenanters** took over Scotland. A covenant is an agreement. The Covenanters agreed to stick together and defend the Presbyterian Church. In 1639 Charles attacked with an English army. The Scots won easily. Charles could not raise a better army without a lot of money. He could not get more money without a Parliament. So in 1640 he called his first Parliament for eleven years, to get enough money to raise an army to fight the Scots Covenanters.

29 April 1639 Our army is weak; our purse is weaker. If we fight with these forces early in the year, we shall have our throats cut. If we delay fighting long, we cannot, for want of money, keep our army together. I dare say there was never so raw, so unskilful and so unwilling an army brought to fight. As yet they are as like to kill their fellows as the enemy.

From a letter by Sir Edmund Verney, Charles I's standard bearer, who was with the army raised to fight the Scots in 1639.

Driuinge Men Women & children by hundreds vpon Briges & casting them into Riuers, who drowned not were killed with poles & shot with muskets.

M.r Blandry Minister hanged after pulled his flesh from his bones in his wiffes sight

A 17th-century print about the Irish Rebellion.

Ireland

In **Ireland** most of the poorer people, and many of the rich, were Catholics. The country was divided between Catholics and Protestants, and also between recent English and Scots settlers and the Irish who had been there for a long time. The English and Scots settlers were usually Protestants. There had been rebellions against English rule and against Protestantism.

Charles I sent one of his best ministers, the **Earl of Strafford**, to rule Ireland. Strafford was a success. He got the Catholics and Protestants to co-operate. He made sure the Irish Parliament always agreed with his policies. He even raised a strong army in Ireland, which could have been used to fight for Charles against the Scots. But this army worried many people in England. Strafford wanted Charles to rule without a Parliament in England. His Irish army was mainly Catholic. Many English people were scared that Charles might use Strafford's army against them.

The second English Parliament which met in 1640 (the **Long Parliament**) arrested Strafford and tried him for treason. With Strafford gone, a rebellion broke out in Ireland. It was a Catholic rebellion, and many Protestants were murdered. Charles needed to raise an army to put down this rebellion.

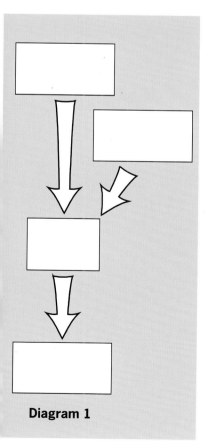

Diagram 1

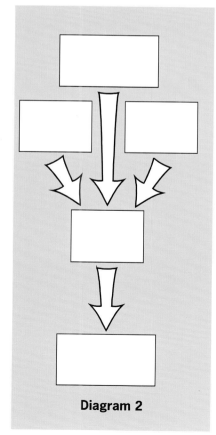

Diagram 2

Questions

Section A

1 Does Source A prove the riot was about the new prayer book? Explain your answer.

2 a What does Source B tell you about Charles's army in 1639?
 b Do you think Sir Edmund Verney is likely to be a reliable witness? Give reasons for your answer.

3 Are the people being ill-treated in Source C Protestants or Catholics?

4 What did the artist of Source C want people to think about the Irish Rebellion? Give reasons for your answer.

Section B

5 Copy Diagram 1 into your book. Fill in the labels from the choices below.
 ● rebellion
 ● Charles wanted new church services
 ● most Scots wanted to keep their Presbyterian Church
 ● Charles needed to raise an army.

6 Were all the causes of the Scottish Rebellion equally important? Give reasons for your answer.

7 Copy Diagram 2 into your book. Fill in the labels from the choices below.
 ● rebellion
 ● many Irish disliked English rule
 ● many Irish were Catholics
 ● Charles needed to raise an army
 ● the Irish were ruled harshly by Strafford.

8 Make a key and shade in different ways boxes which are **causes**, **motives** and **consequences**. Are there any boxes that are either two or all three? Explain why.

9 How many causes do you think there were for the Irish Rebellion: one, three or four? Explain your answer.

5.4 The Start of the Civil War

Charles I had to call a Parliament in 1640 to get money to raise an army to fight the Scots. It met on 13 April, the first Parliament for eleven years. Charles soon quarrelled with it. Parliament insisted on discussing its **grievances** (the things it didn't like about the way Charles had run the country) before voting money for the war. He dissolved it on 5 May. Historians call it the **Short Parliament**.

Charles decided to go to war against the Scots anyway. It was a disaster. Not only could the Scots keep Charles out of Scotland, but they also invaded northern England. The Scots agreed to return to Scotland, but only if Charles paid all the costs of their army as well as his. Until then, the Scots army stayed in England. This meant Charles had to call another Parliament. Only taxes voted by Parliament would give him enough money to pay off the Scots.

The Long Parliament

The **Long Parliament** (so called because it sat until 1653) first met in November 1640. Charles could not dissolve it because he needed taxes to pay off the Scots. MPs, led by **John Pym**, made it clear that they would only vote taxes after the grievances had been settled. He wanted to make sure no king could ever rule again without calling Parliament. Charles's two chief ministers, Strafford and Laud, were imprisoned, and Strafford was soon executed for treason.

Parliament forced Charles to agree to many reforms. The most important were a law that there must be a Parliament at least once every three years, and that Charles could not end the Long Parliament until it agreed. He also accepted that most of his schemes to get money during the 11 Years Tyranny were illegal.

It is important to realize that nobody wanted a civil war when Parliament first met. Pym and his allies wanted Parliament to be much more important. Most MPs wanted the sort of things that had gone on between 1629 and 1640 to stop. Charles wanted to keep as much power as he could, and also defend the Church of England against the Puritans. Many Puritans wanted the Church of England to change, and to be allowed to set up their own churches and worship in their own way. Most people had got most of what they wanted by the summer of 1641. Why, then, was there a civil war? The problem for Pym and his supporters was simple. Could they trust Charles to keep his side of the bargain?

Source A

Title page of a pamphlet, published in 1642.

Questions

Section A

1 a Draw a timeline showing the events of 1640–42.
  b Mark on the timeline the point when you think the Civil War became something that was likely to happen.
  c Give reasons for your choice.

2 In the 17th century, people counted the new year from March not January. Printers often used an 'f' for an 's'. Who were the 'Five Members' in Pym's speech (Source A)?

3 Which tells you more about Charles's attempt to arrest the Five Members, Source A or B?

The Irish Rebellion

While Parliament were worrying about whether they could trust Charles, the Irish Rebellion started. People were shocked by the news of the killing in Ireland. The Irish rebels claimed that Charles approved of their rebellion, although this was not true. Even people who did not think Charles was involved in the Irish Rebellion wondered if he could be trusted with an army to put it down. He might use it to get rid of the English Parliament first.

On 4 January 1642 he tried to arrest the **Five Members** – his leading opponents in Parliament. They had already left the House, but this action came as a great shock. How could Parliament discuss the country's problems if the king might force his way in with armed men and arrest people who criticized him?

Crowds in London demonstrated in defence of Parliament. Charles thought it would be safer to leave the city. In February the queen went abroad to raise money for Charles. In April Sir John Hotham, a supporter of Parliament, would not let Charles into Hull, where all the arms from the war with Scotland were stored. In June both sides started to raise soldiers, and on 22 August Charles I raised his standard, the traditional declaration of war.

Source B

Charles I in Parliament, during his attempt to arrest the Five Members. This picture is a still from a modern film, 'Cromwell'.

Section B

4 Make your own diagram of the causes of the Civil War, like the diagrams of the causes of the Irish and Scottish Rebellions on page 53. Give it a key and shade the causes and consequences differently.

5 What did the following people want when the Long Parliament first met:
a John Pym; **b** most MPs;
c Charles I.

6 There was a civil war. Does this mean that what people wanted did not matter at all? Explain your answer.

5.5 The Civil War

1642

The first great battle of the Civil War, **Edgehill,** in 1642, was a draw. Later, Charles tried to capture London, and got as far as Turnham Green (now a station on the London Underground). There, however, his army was so outnumbered by Parliament's forces that he retreated without fighting. He withdrew to Oxford for the winter.

1643

Charles planned a triple attack on London with his armies from the north, the west and Oxford. The plan failed. Each army was held up trying to capture towns in their own areas. That winter Parliament made a treaty with the **Scots**. In return for help from the Scottish army, Parliament agreed to set up a Scots-style Presbyterian Church in England.

1644

Parliament had a chance to win the war. At **Marston Moor** the Scots, together with two of Parliament's armies, beat **Prince Rupert** and destroyed his army. Until then, Rupert had been the most successful Royalist general. In the south, Parliament sent two armies to defeat the king and capture Oxford. But their generals would not work together, and Charles was able to beat each separately. Charles's success in the south evened out his loss in the north.

Source A

Parts of a painted glass window from a church in Cheshire, made about 1646. The window was a memorial to soldiers who had fought in the Civil War siege of Chester.

Source B

Some of the fighting positions for pikemen and musketeers. These are taken from a civil war 'drill book' used to train soldiers.

Source C

A print showing Royalist soldiers, published by supporters of Parliament during the war.

1645

During the winter there were bitter quarrels in Parliament. The generals, who were mainly members of the House of Commons or House of Lords, blamed one another for not winning the war in 1644. Eventually Parliament decided to scrap the old armies, and most of the old generals. The **New Model Army** was set up. MPs and lords were banned from holding commands in this army. The new commander, **Sir Thomas Fairfax**, got a special permission for one MP, **Oliver Cromwell**, to lead the cavalry.

The Royalists were scornful of the New Model Army, and were keen to fight. Despite being outnumbered about 9,000 to 14,000, they attacked at **Naseby**. Parliament's forces won. Cromwell and the cavalry made the decisive breakthrough; they defeated the Royalist cavalry and then attacked the Royalist infantry from behind. The battle was soon over, with the Royalist infantry destroyed. About 4,500 were prisoners, and the rest were dead.

Naseby was the end of the king's last great army. The New Model Army beat the only other large Royalist force at the battle of **Langport**, before capturing **Bristol**, the Royalists' second most important city. **Oxford** was not captured until 1646, but from Naseby onwards there could be little doubt who would win the war.

Questions

Section A

1 Write a paragraph about the events of each year of the war from 1642 to 1645.

2 Are the sources in this unit **primary** or **secondary** sources for historians studying the Civil War?

Section B

3 There were two types of foot soldiers during the Civil War: pikemen and musketeers. Source A also shows some soldiers' equipment. Which type of soldier used each of the pieces of equipment numbered below?

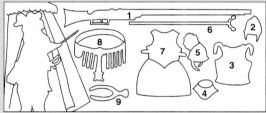

4 Which source, or part of a source, would help you explain the following statements about fighting during the Civil War?
   a Musketeers took nearly two minutes to load and fire.
   b Pikemen were usually larger and stronger men than musketeers.

5 a What are the soldiers doing in Source C?
   b Is there any reason to think this source might not be completely reliable? Explain your answer.

6 Sources A, B and C all show pikemen. Do these sources **support** or **contradict** one another?

7 How were pikemen armed during the Civil War? Support your answer with reference to the sources and explain why the sources have helped you reach your conclusions.

5.6 The Trial and Execution of Charles I

Charles I was not the first English king to be killed by his subjects. Edward II and Richard II had been quietly murdered. Charles, however, was put on trial, found guilty, and **publicly executed**. This was a very different sort of king-killing.

In 1647 Charles was a prisoner of Parliament. But Parliament was split into different groups. Charles tried to negotiate with all of them. At the same time, he secretly planned a new civil war. He arranged for the Scots to change sides. In 1648 their army invaded England to fight for Charles. There were also Royalist uprisings in various parts of England.

This **Second Civil War** was soon over. The New Model Army was too strong for both the Scots and the Royalists. The generals, especially Cromwell, blamed Charles for all the death and injury because his plotting had caused the war. Also, they felt that Charles could not be trusted. He had started a second war, and he might well try a third. The only way to be safe was to get rid of Charles.

The **Presbyterians** in Parliament could not imagine England without a king or queen. After the war they made a deal with Charles called the **Treaty of Newport**. This would have given Charles many of his old powers back, almost as if the civil wars had not happened. This was too much for the New Model Army. If Parliament could not be trusted to deal with Charles, the army would have to deal with Parliament.

The result was **Pride's Purge** on 6 December 1648. Colonel Pride stood outside the House of Commons with some soldiers. He stopped most Presbyterian MPs from going in, and arrested their leaders. Those MPs who were left, called the **Rump**, soon agreed that Charles should be put on trial for his crimes. They appointed a special **High Court of Justice**, because no ordinary court had the power to try a king. Charles was accused of being 'a tyrant, traitor and murderer, and a public and implacable enemy to the Commonwealth of England'. Charles would not accept that the court had the power to try him. The court went ahead, however, and he was found guilty and sentenced to death by beheading.

The execution was on 30 January 1649. There was a large crowd, but they had to wait while Parliament passed another Act saying it was illegal to proclaim a new king. Charles was very brave, asking the executioner to wait until he had finished praying. His head was cut off with one blow.

Source A

The special hat that Richard Bradshaw, the judge at Charles's trial, had made for himself. It was reinforced with metal.

Source B

On the day of his execution, which was Tuesday 30 January, I stood among the crowd in the street before Whitehall Gate, where the scaffold was erected, and saw what was done. The blow I saw given, and I remember well, there was such a groan by the thousands then present, as I never heard before and desire I may never hear again. Troops were sent to control the people, and to disperse and scatter them, so that I had much ado among the rest to escape home without hurt.

From the diary of Philip Henry, a young man with a Royalist background.

Activities

1 Does Source A prove that the trial of Charles I was unpopular?

2 a How does Source B suggest the army thought there might be trouble at the execution?

   b Does Source C support this?

3 Does Source C suggest the execution was popular or unpopular?

4 Can you say, judging by these sources, whether the trial and execution of Charles were popular?

Source C

The execution of Charles in 1649, from a painting of the time.

Questions

Section A

1 Copy out the following paragraph, choosing the better alternative from the words in *italics*.

When he was a prisoner in 1647 Charles *dealt fairly with/double-crossed* the army and the Presbyterians. He got the *Scots/ Presbyterians* to start another war, fighting on his side. After the *Royalists/New Model Army* lost the war, Charles made a deal with the *Royalists/Presbyterians* called the Treaty of Newport. This *pleased/upset* the army. Pride's Purge cleared the *Presbyterians/ Royalists* out of Parliament. The *Rump/Army* then ordered the *trial/trial and execution* of Charles.

Section B

2
- The Second Civil War.
- The Treaty of Newport.
- Pride's Purge.
- Charles found guilty by the High Court of Justice.

Historians have suggested all the above were **causes** of Charles I's execution. Do you agree? Explain your answer.

3 Some causes **make it possible** for something else to happen. These are called **enabling causes** because they enable something to happen. Which of the causes in the list above is an enabling cause? Give reasons for your answer.

4 Are all the causes on the list equally important in explaining why Charles I was executed? Give reasons for your answer.

5 Suggest two other causes of Charles's execution.

5.7 Commonwealth and Protectorate

The king was dead. On 17 March 1649 the Rump **abolished the monarchy** altogether. Kings, it said, were 'unnecessary, burdensome and dangerous to the liberty, safety and public interest of the people'. The Rump set up the **Commonwealth** as a **republic**. Its rulers were to be elected by at least some of the people. The Rump was to be the Commonwealth's first Parliament. New elections were promised later.

The new Commonwealth had enemies. Many powerful Irish, Scots and English people were Catholics, or Royalists, or both. But the Commonwealth had the New Model Army on its side. General Fairfax retired, and **Oliver Cromwell** took over. In the next three years, the army beat the Irish, the Scots and the English Royalists.

Many people at the time thought that God affected events. Victors in a war often claimed they won because God was on their side. They called this **God's providence**. Cromwell and much of his army were Puritans. They claimed that the victories from Naseby onwards proved that God was on their side. They expected the Rump to make England a more godly country, run according to Puritan ideas.

The Rump did not make the sort of reforms which the army and its supporters wanted. In April 1653 it even discussed a new idea for elections where the existing members of the Rump would not have to be re-elected. This was too much for Cromwell. With his soldiers, he went to the Houses of Parliament. He listened to the debate for a while, then stood up and said to the Rump: 'You have sat here long enough.' He called in his soldiers and cleared the House.

Barebone's Parliament

Cromwell and the army did not want to turn the country into a military dictatorship – they saw themselves as fighting for freedom. But they could not be sure that elections would choose MPs with the same ideas as they had. They set up a Parliament where the members were nominated rather than elected. Cromwell and his advisers had the final say about who would sit, but they asked for suggestions from churches and other groups around the country. This Parliament first met on 4 July 1653. It is usually called **Barebone's Parliament** after the name of one of its members, Praise-God Barebone.

The case of James Nayler

The Parliament of 1656 also quarrelled with Cromwell about James Nayler. Nayler had re-enacted Christ's entry into Jerusalem on Palm Sunday. In Nayler's case he entered Bristol, with women strewing the ground in front of him with leaves and clothes. Parliament was horrified. It decided that Nayler ought to be punished and had him brought to London. Parliament made itself accuser, judge and jury. It found Nayler guilty and discussed the death penalty. Finally it decided on a 'milder' punishment. Nayler was to be put in the pillory, be publicly whipped, have his tongue bored through with a red-hot iron, be branded with a 'B' (for blasphemer) on the forehead, be taken to Bristol, be publicly whipped again and be returned to London and kept in prison until Parliament decided to let him out.

To Cromwell this did not look much like the freedom and liberty he had spent the last fifteen years fighting for. Parliament could be just as much a tyrant as Charles had been. The constitution had limited his powers as Protector, but it had not limited the power of Parliament enough.

There were a number of **radicals** (people who wanted a lot of changes) in Barebone's Parliament. There were also plenty of moderate gentlemen, from the families whose men traditionally became MPs. The radicals were careful to go to every debate, and they often won the votes even though most MPs were not radicals. The moderates were so worried by this that they made sure they all turned up early on 12 December 1653. They voted to dissolve Parliament and gave power back to Cromwell.

The Protectorate

For the second time in a year Cromwell had total power over Britain. He set up a government called the **Protectorate** with a new **constitution** (a set of rules to say how the country should be run). The Protectorate was more like the old monarchy. At the head of the government was the **Protector** (Cromwell himself). The Protector had the sort of power the Long Parliament had wanted to give Charles I. There was also to be a Parliament at least once every three years. To make sure Parliament had the 'right' sort of ideas, ex-Royalists were banned from voting.

Parliaments found plenty to criticize under the Protectorate. The first one, in 1654, tried to change the constitution. Cromwell did not agree and eventually dismissed the Parliament. The second Parliament, in 1656, wanted Cromwell to become king. He refused. Many people in the country wanted to get back to the old ways, and liked the idea of having a king; but Cromwell and many of the army could not forget they had fought wars to stop England having one.

Despite these disagreements while Oliver Cromwell lived, the Protectorate was fairly successful. The country was well governed. European countries, especially France and Spain, feared Britain's power and tried to get Cromwell to join them in their wars against each other.

Source A

A print from the time showing Cromwell dismissing the Rump Parliament.

Questions

Section A

1 Who do you think the following people in Source A are?

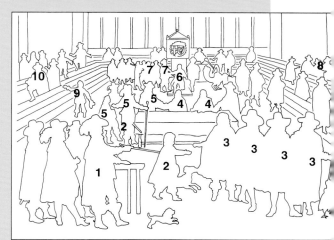

2 Some historians have said that Cromwell was ambitious and power-hungry. Others have said he was not. Use the information in this unit to answer the question: **Was Cromwell after power for himself?** Try to give some reasons which would support the answer 'yes' and some which would support the answer 'no'. Then come to a conclusion.

Section B

3 How did the following groups affect events between 1649 and 1656:
   ● the army   ● Parliament
   ● Royalists   ● Puritans?

4 'The MPs who sentenced Nayler were Christians and they didn't think they were being cruel.' Can this be true? Explain your answer.

61

5.8 The Restoration

Source A

Next morning the Council ordered the proclamation of Richard as Lord Protector to be made at ten o'clock at Whitehall. The proclamation was followed by loud cries of 'God save the Lord Protector!' and great applause at Whitehall, Westminster, Temple Bar, Cheapside and the Royal Exchange in Cornhill. In Exeter, on 6 September, the magistrates and Council proclaimed Richard. When this had been done, the crowd shouted: 'amen, amen, God preserve my Lord Richard, Lord Protector!' The proclamation caused equal enthusiasm throughout England. Sometimes wine and beer were distributed free; sometimes volleys of shots, the ringing of bells, bonfires and 'treats' were features of the celebrations.

From Godfrey Davies, 'The Restoration of Charles II', 1955.

Source B

Charles II arrived at Dover at about two o'clock in the afternoon. Ready on the shore to receive him stood the Lord General Monk, the Constable of Dover Castle, many persons of quality and the mayor of Dover. From there he went to Barham Down, where multitudes of the country people stood, making loud shouts. He rode to the head of each group of them, who, bowing to him, kissed the hilts of their swords, then waved them above their heads, with no less shouting. At Canterbury the mayor and aldermen received him with loud music, and presented him with a cup of gold, worth £250. In magnificent fashion his majesty entered the city of London at the Bridge; where he found the windows and streets exceedingly thronged with people to see him. The walls were decorated with hangings of tapestry and other costly stuff. All the fountains, as he passed, ran with claret wine.

From 'England's Joy', 1660, describing the return of Charles II.

Oliver Cromwell died on 3 September 1658. His son, **Richard**, succeeded him as Lord Protector. Source A shows how popular this was. Oliver was given an expensive state funeral in Westminster Abbey. Less than two years later, however, enthusiastic crowds welcomed **Charles II** back to England (Source B).

Oliver Cromwell's body was dug up and taken to Tyburn, where public hangings took place. Also taken were the bodies of Ireton (his son-in-law) and Bradshaw (the judge at Charles I's trial). The bodies were hanged. After a couple of hours they were taken down and beheaded. The headless bodies were thrown into an unmarked pit, and the heads were stuck on spikes outside Whitehall. They stayed there until they were blown down in a gale about 20 years later. What had happened to change so much so quickly?

The republic collapsed. Richard Cromwell had not been able to control the army. He was soon replaced by the **Rump Parliament**. The Rump and the army still could not get on. The army expelled the Rump again, and then soon accepted it back. Most people were unhappy with all the changes. They wanted a strong and fair government. After Oliver's death, nobody could supply it.

Eventually **General Monk**, commander of the army in Scotland, marched to London. His part of the army was probably the strongest, and it was loyal to him. The army in England was split with quarrels about politics and religion.

Questions

Section A

1 Write out these lists in their correct chronological order.
   a Rump Parliament restored; Declaration of Breda; Oliver Cromwell died; Monk marched to London.
   b Richard Cromwell proclaimed Protector in Exeter; Richard Cromwell resigned from the Protectorship; Richard Cromwell proclaimed Protector in London; Oliver Cromwell died.

2 Why do you think the bodies of Cromwell, Ireton and Bradshaw were dug up and disfigured?

3 Do the sources in this unit prove that everyone was pleased when the monarchy was restored in 1660?

4 Does Source D prove the text is correct when it says that some regicides were executed in a most brutal way?

When Monk arrived in London he decided to restore the **Long Parliament**. This meant bringing back as many of the original MPs of 1640 as were still around. Ex-Royalists came back to the House of Commons, as did the Presbyterians driven out by Pride's Purge in 1648. Monk knew that a House with these men in it would try to restore Charles I's son.

There were still major problems to be solved before Charles II could return. The main questions were:

● What would happen about the Church? Would the Church of England be the only one allowed, or would Puritans be allowed to set up their own churches?

● What would happen to all the people who had fought against Charles I? Would they be punished?

● What would happen to all the land which had been confiscated from Royalists and from the king? Much of it had been sold to raise money.

● Would the soldiers get the pay that they were still owed?

Charles II's answer to these problems was the **Declaration of Breda**. In it, he said he would accept Parliament's suggestions about all four problems.

Most people who had supported Parliament in the Civil Wars were left alone after the **Restoration**. The **regicides** (those who had signed the death warrant of Charles I) were persecuted. Some fled abroad, some were assassinated, and some refused to flee. They were tried and executed in a most brutal way.

Source C

An English plate, made at the time of the Restoration (1660).

Source D

A print sold at the time, showing the execution of four regicides in 1661.

Section B

5 a Did the army in London want Charles II back?

b Did the actions of the London army help cause the Restoration?

6 Was the Declaration of Breda likely to help Charles II get back the throne?

7 Was the loyalty of Monk's soldiers to him a **cause** of the Restoration?

8 Make up your own **cause-and-effect** diagram for the Restoration. Use these labels for the boxes:

Army not willing to accept government it didn't like.

Army became more unpopular.

Charles II popular.

Monk wanted strong and fair government.

Declaration of Breda.

Use more boxes if you think there should be more factors in the diagram. Use arrows to show the connections between causes and effects, and shade boxes differently to show causes, effects and motives. Some factors might be both cause and effect.

5.9 *The Great Plague*

Plague struck London many times during the 17th century. By far the worst occasion was the **Great Plague of 1665**.

Doctors did not know what caused the plague. Some thought it was caused by the position of the planets. Most thought it was caught by touch or from bad smells. London had no proper drains or sewers, so the streets were filthy, and there were many rats. There were plenty of bad smells in London as well. Other people thought it was a punishment from God – people could think this and also think that it was spread by bad smells. We now know that plague was most often spread by the fleas from the rats which lived in the filthy city.

There were no successful medical treatments for the plague. **Isolation** was the main treatment – shutting the sick up until they either died or got better. This didn't really help the sick people, but it might have stopped them spreading the plague to others. The rich left London. They only returned when the weekly **bills of mortality** (lists of the dead) showed that the plague was more or less over.

Those who stayed in London were worried about touching things which might have been touched by the sick. Shopkeepers kept dishes of vinegar on their counters. They would not take money from their customers. The customers dropped the coins in the vinegar and then the shopkeeper picked them up. Shoppers would pick up what they wanted themselves, not be handed things by the shopkeeper. Most people carried 'posies' of sweet-smelling herbs and flowers. If they could not afford posies, they carried cloth soaked in vinegar.

Source A

London's bill of mortality for 1665.

Source B

Examiners
to enquire what houses in every parish be visited by the Plague, what persons be sick and of what diseases. If they find one sick of the Plague, to give order to the Constable that the house be shut up.

Searchers
Women-Searchers be sworn to make search and true report whether the persons do die of the Plague. No Searcher be permitted to keep any shop or stall, or be employed as a laundress.

Doctors
to join with Searchers to view the body, that there may be a true report made of the disease.

Isolation of the Sick
As soon as any be found to be sick of the Plague, they shall be shut in their house, and the house shut for a month.

Burial of the Dead
be always either before sun-rising or after sun-setting. No neighbours or friends be suffered to accompany the corpse to church, or enter the dead person's house, on pain of having their own house shut up. All graves shall be at least six feet deep.

Every Visited House
to be marked with a red cross a foot long, in the middle of the door, and with these usual printed words: 'Lord Have Mercy Upon Us'.

Every Visited House
to be watched by watchmen who shall get necessaries unto them.

The streets to be kept clean
and the filth of houses be daily carried away. That no hogs, dogs, cats, tame pigeons or rabbits be kept within the city, or any pigs in the streets or lanes.

Orders of the Lord Mayor of London concerning the plague, 1665.

Source C

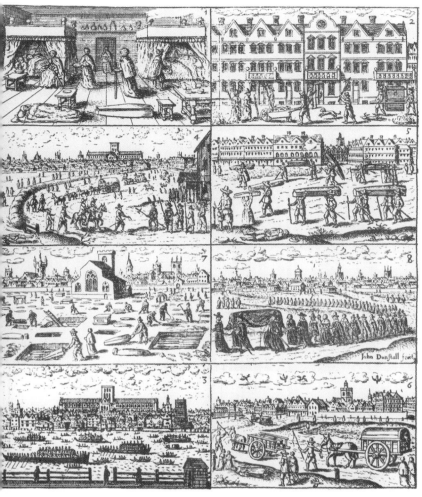

Scenes from a print sold at the time, showing London during the plague.

Source D

7 June. This day I did in Drury Lane see two or three houses marked with a red cross upon the doors and 'Lord Have Mercy Upon Us' writ there. It put me into an ill conception of myself and my smell, so that I was forced to buy some roll tobacco to smell and chew – which took away the worry.

10 June. Home to bed – being troubled at the sickness, and my head filled with business enough, particularly how to put my things and estate in good order, in case it should please God to call me away.

16 October But Lord how empty the streets are, and melancholy, so many poor sick people in the streets, full of sores. Everybody talking of this dead and that man sick, and so many in this place and so many in that.

Entries in Samuel Pepys's Diary during summer and autumn, 1665.

Questions

Section A

1 Copy out the following sentences. Match up each 'tail' with the correct 'head'.

Heads	Tails
a Plague was a common problem	what caused it.
b Doctors did not know	by bad smells, others by touch.
c Some thought it was spread	to stop them spreading it.
d If people had the plague they were shut up	not touching things others had touched and carrying posies.
e People tried to avoid the plague by leaving London,	in 17th-century London.

2 a How people many died from the plague in 1665?
  b How many people died from it in 1664?
  c Does Source A suggest that medicine has improved since 1665?

3 a Why were the 'Searchers' not allowed to have shops (Source B)?
  b How did the mayor think the plague was spread (Source B)?

4 Do Sources C and D suggest that historians can rely on Source B to tell them about London during the plague?

Section B

5 What effect did the following features of life in the 17th century have on the plague:
  ● lack of medical knowledge
  ● religious beliefs
  ● poor sanitation (drains and sewers)?

6 Sniffing vinegar-soaked cloth will not stop you catching the plague. Why did people do it?

5.10 The Great Fire of London

Source A

> 2 September. Walked to the Tower and there got up on one of the high places. I did see the houses at that end of the bridge all on fire, and an infinite great fire on this and the other side of the end of the bridge. The Lieutenant of the Tower tells me it began this morning in the King's-baker's house in Pudding Lane. Everybody endeavouring to remove their goods, and flinging into the River or bringing them into boats. Poor people staying in their houses as long as till the very fire touched them, and then running into boats. I stayed, and in an hour's time saw the fire rage every way, and nobody to my sight trying to quench it, but to remove their goods and leave all to the fire. The wind mighty high and driving it into the city, and everything, after so long a drought, proving combustible. [Later] It being darkish we saw the fire as one entire arch of fire from this to the other side of the bridge. It made me weep to see it. The churches, houses and all on fire and flaming at once, and a horrid noise the flames made, and the crackling of houses at their ruin. So home with a sad heart.

From Samuel Pepys's Diary for 1666.

The **Great Fire of London** was such a terrible disaster that many people at the time could not believe it was an accident. A Catholic plot was suspected. People fleeing from London spread the rumour. Catholics were attacked in the streets. One was nearly killed when a crowd thought he was carrying fire-balls. They turned out to be tennis balls.

Henry Young, a distiller (beer- or wine-maker), claimed that a Jesuit had told him in 1661 that within seven years all England would be Catholic. Young replied that the City of London 'would never endure it'. The Jesuit answered that within five or six years they would 'break the power and strength of London in pieces'.

Robert Hubert, a Frenchman, who claimed to be a Catholic, was arrested for starting the fire. He confessed, and was able to show where the house had been in which the fire had started. He was executed on 27 October.

The Great Fire is an example of an incident where many people at the time believed something different to the view of most historians. Why should historians' views be so different? Is it because they are further away and less influenced by emotion? Or have the details of the story got confused over time?

Source B

The Monument. This column was built in 1669 near the baker's shop in Pudding Lane where the Great Fire started. The inscription says that the fire was started by Catholics.

Source C

A modern model of the Fire of London.

Source D

The year of 1666 is notable for the Fire of London. A number of accidents combined to make this an unusually great disaster. It happened in the autumn, when many merchants had gone into the country, and tradesmen were away collecting their rents. It broke out in a street where there were stores of things likely to burn, such as pitch, tar and rope. A wind from the east blew the fire towards the centre of the city, and the water pump at the north end of London Bridge happened at the time to be out of order. As the season was dry and the wells at their lowest, the fire blazed unchecked for several days.

From David Ogg, 'England in the Reign of Charles II', 1956.

Robert Latham, a modern historian, writing in 1974.

Source E

Robert Hubert, a London watchmaker who was born in France, was tried in October 1666 and executed on the 27th of that month. The only evidence against him was his own confession, which he later denied. It does not appear to be true that he was a Catholic, as he claimed. The fact that he was able to identify the site of the baker's house proved nothing since for a long time it had been on public show. He was in fact mentally disordered and had landed in London from Sweden two days after the fire had started.

Source F

5 November. Sir Thomas Crew says, from what he has heard at the Committee for investigating the burning of the City, that it was certainly done by a plot – it being proved by many witnesses that attempts were made in several places to increase the fire. Both in the City and the country several Papists boasted that on such a day or in such a time we should find the hottest weather that ever was in England.

From Samuel Pepys's Diary for 1666.

Questions

Section A

1 Will historians studying the Great Fire find Source B useful? Explain your answer.

2 a Why, according to David Ogg (Source D), did the Great Fire burn so much of London?
  b Should an historian accept Ogg's reasons as an explanation for this? Give reasons for your answer.

Section B

3 Make a list of the statements of **fact**, and the statements of **opinion**, in Sources D and E.

4 Does Source D disprove the theory that Robert Hubert started the Great Fire? Give reasons for your answer.

5 ● Robert Hubert pleaded guilty to starting the Great Fire and was hanged for it.
  ● In 1667 the House of Commons committee investigating the Great Fire decided it had been started by Catholics.
  ● In 1669 the Monument was built with an inscription saying the fire was started by Catholics.
  No modern historian believes in a Catholic plot to start the Great Fire. Why should modern historians' views be so different from those of people at the time?

5.11 Science and Superstition

There were many advances in **scientific knowledge** in the 17th century. In 1628 **William Harvey** was able to prove that the heart pumped the same blood round and round the body. Before Harvey, people had thought that blood was a bit like petrol. It was always being used up; new blood being made and taken to the parts of the body where it was needed. Harvey took great care to prove his ideas with **experiments**. People could try these for themselves and see that his ideas were right.

Finding ways to test and prove theories to be true was the key to the new scientific thinking. In the second half of the 17th century many of the world leaders in the new science were English. The **Royal Society** was set up as a place where scientists could meet and discuss one another's ideas. Its greatest member was **Isaac Newton** who was able to explain how the solar system worked. He reduced the complex movements of all the planets to a mathematical equation. He proved his ideas by showing that his equation could be used to **predict** where the planets would be in the future as well as **explain** where they had been in the past.

Source A

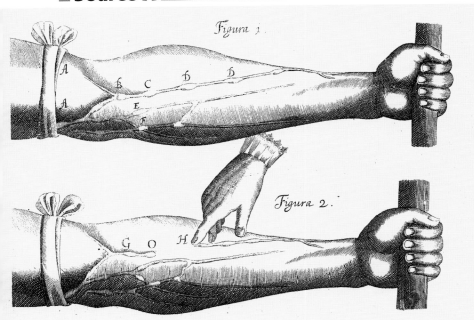

Diagrams from William Harvey's book showing how blood travels through the veins, 1628.

Source B

Title page of a 17th-century book on witchcraft.

Source C

> Every old woman with a wrinkled face, a furr'd brow, a hairy lip, a gobber tooth, a squint eye, a squeaking voice or a scolding tongue is pronounced a witch.

Reverend John Gaule, 1646.

Source D

People queuing to be touched by King Charles II. They hoped his touch would cure them of the disease scrofula.

Britain was not a completely rational place in the 17th century, however. Belief in God and the Devil were the way that many people explained events in their daily lives. Source D shows King Charles II touching people to cure them of an illness. If people believed illnesses had supernatural causes, they were likely to believe in supernatural cures.

Most British people believed that God was actively involved in the day-to-day events of their world. They also believed that the Devil was active, working against God. If beer went sour or a cow fell sick most people looked for a supernatural explanation, not a natural one. **Witches** were thought to be people who had made a contract with the Devil. The Devil would give them special powers during their life, in return for their soul when they died.

In England and Wales suspected witches were not tortured. If they were found guilty they were hanged. In Scotland suspected witches could be tortured, and if they were found guilty they were burned. Not all court records have survived from the 17th century, but historians have studied many that have. People accused of being witches have a number of things in common. They were usually poor and quite old, over 40 at least. Nine out of ten were women, and most of them were widows. They were often people who would depend on charity to live.

Questions

Section A

1 a What did Harvey discover?
  b What was important about the way he discovered it?
  c Why is Source A important?
  d How did the Royal Society help the spread of science?
  e What did Newton discover?
  f What are the similarities between Newton and Harvey?

2 a What sorts of things did people believe witches could do?
  b How were witches thought to have got their power?
  c Why might there have been more witches convicted in Scotland than England?

Section B

3 Do you think it is likely that Newton believed in witches?

4 There were more witchcraft prosecutions in England and Scotland in some years than others. Poor harvests or times of great trouble like the late 1640s were the times with most prosecutions. Why might this have been?

5.12 The Glorious Revolution

James II

When **Charles II** died in 1685 he was succeeded by his brother, **James II**. James was a Catholic. Most people in Britain were not. Many thought that the Catholic religion was against their ideas of liberty. However, people were prepared to put up with James. He was an old man, not likely to be king for long, and his children, both girls, were Protestants. People remembered the troubles between 1640 and 1660 and they wanted a quiet life.

James, however, didn't want a quiet life. He wanted to change the country and improve the position of Catholics. He claimed the power to **suspend laws**. He started off by suspending the laws against the Catholics. When the **judges** didn't agree, he sacked most of them and appointed new ones. The new ones said he could suspend any law he liked. He also sacked most **magistrates** who didn't agree with him.

In 1688 James's new young wife had a son. A son would inherit the crown before the older daughters, and would be brought up a Catholic. A group of the most powerful men in the country invited **William of Orange**, husband of James's eldest daughter, **Mary**, from the Netherlands to help them oppose the king. William landed with an army on 5 November 1688. He said he would accept any decision about the future that Parliament made. James's army deserted, and James fled to France.

Source A

King James, having tried to subvert the constitution of the kingdom by breaking the contract between King and People, and by the advice of Jesuits and other wicked persons having violated [broken] the fundamental laws, and having withdrawn himself out of the kingdom, has abdicated the government. And the throne is thereby vacant.

Resolution of the House of Commons, 1689

Political changes: 1603–88. Mobs in the towns and cities were quick to riot when they felt they were losing their freedoms. The Popish Soap riots are a good example. Landowners rioted in the 1630s against the high price and poor quality of 'official' soap. Charles I had given the licence to make this soap to a group which included a number of Catholics. This group used the law to try to drive other soap manufacturers out of business.

Parliament's Bill of Rights

When William arrived in London he called a parliament. There was some argument about what should happen, but the arguments were solved by a **resolution** of the House of Commons. It was cleverly worded to appeal to Catholics, people who wanted a powerful monarchy and people who wanted a powerful parliament.

Parliament agreed that the throne was vacant and then decided who should sit on it. It offered the throne to William and Mary jointly, but only if they accepted Parliament's conditions. The conditions became known as the **Bill of Rights**. Together with some Acts of Parliament passed soon after, this solved some of the questions that parliaments and kings had argued about since 1603.

The revolution settlement

● **Religion** The monarch could not be, or marry, a Catholic. Protestants who did not want to join the Church of England could have their own churches. However, the right to vote and the right to become an MP would only be given to men who were members of the Church of England.

● **Parliament** Only Parliament could grant taxes and pass laws. There must be a new Parliament at least once every three years.

● **The law** The monarch could not suspend laws. Only Parliament could repeal (cancel) a law. Only Parliament could set up special courts to try particular cases.

● **Money** The cost of running the country was separated from the monarch's own finances. There was to be a special payment, the **Civil List**, to cover the monarch's personal expenses.

● **The army** Control over the army was to be shared. The monarch would be the head of the army; but Parliament would have to pass an Act each year to give the power to keep discipline in the army.

The **Glorious Revolution of 1688–9** marked a **shift in power** between monarch and Parliament. Parliament was now the more powerful of the two. James I's idea of the 'divine right of kings' was clearly finished. Kings could be appointed by Parliament on the terms that Parliament thought fit.

This does not mean that government suddenly became fair. Most men did not have the right to vote, nor did any women. However, the **idea of some democracy** was safe. Between 1603 and 1689 many countries in Europe had gone through the same problems. In continental Europe it was usually the kings who won. In **France**, for instance, the Estates-General (the equivalent of Britain's Parliament) stopped meeting. The French king had the power to put people in prison without trial, and the power to make whatever laws he wanted. British men and women, by opposing things they thought were not just, had saved their liberty.

Questions

Section A

1 Copy out the following paragraph choosing the best alternative from the words in *italics*.

James II was the *son/brother* of Charles II. James was a *Catholic/Protestant*. James was not a popular king, but people were willing to put up with him until he had *a son/a new idea*. A group of *Protestants/Catholics* invited William of Orange to help them overthrow James. James fled abroad. *Parliament/the Protestant lords* offered the throne to William and his wife, Mary, who was *James's/Charles's* daughter.

2 What were the four main points of the 'revolution settlement'?

Section B

3 Study the cartoon. How was the position of William and Mary as monarchs different from:
   a James I?
   b Charles I?

4 Look back at the powers of Parliament described on page 50–1. Had the power of Parliament changed by 1689?

5 How had life in Britain in the 17th century changed between 1603 and 1689?

6.1 Agriculture, 1750–1914

In 1750 the population of Britain was about 7 million. By 1850 it was 21 million. This meant more people wanting food. The price of food went up. The average price of wheat rose from 35 to 50 shillings per quarter of a hundredweight between 1750 and 1790. Higher prices meant bigger profits for farmers. Many farmers started to look for new methods of farming so that they could produce more and hence make more money.

The open field system

Before 1750 most land was farmed under the **open field system**. Under this system, the cultivated land around a village was divided into three huge open fields. All of the farmers in the area grew their crops on tiny **strips** of land scattered around these fields. Small landowners, called **yeoman farmers**, looked after their own land; bigger landowners rented out strips to **tenant farmers**.

Every year all the farmers would sow one field with wheat, and another field with barley. The third field would be left empty or **fallow** to allow the soil to recover. Farmers also used the **common land**. This was waste land shared by all the villagers to graze their animals or search for wood or wild food.

Enclosures

After 1750, in villages with only a small number of landowners, people sometimes got together and swapped strips so that each owner's land was combined into one area. Each owner could then **enclose** their land with hedges into a farm with several small fields. If they couldn't agree to enclose, landowners could get Parliament to pass an Act to enclose the land. The common land was often included. People got land to match the strips they had owned or to make up for the loss of the common. Between 1750 and 1810 there were over 4,000 Acts, enclosing 5 million acres. They were mainly in the Midlands and the south of England.

Enclosures had some bad effects. They were expensive because of the cost of surveyors' fees and hedging. Some farmers couldn't afford the costs and had to sell their land. Bigger landowners needed fewer tenant farmers. Farm labourers disliked the loss of the free food and firewood from the common.

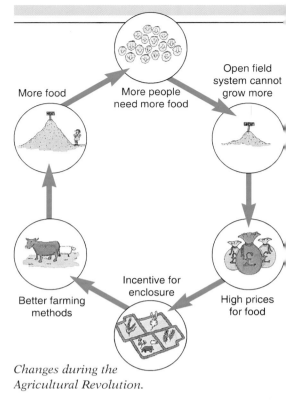

Changes during the Agricultural Revolution.

Source A

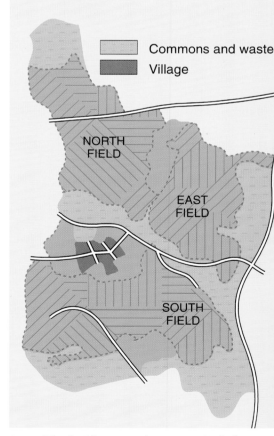

Aston Blank, Gloucestershire, in 1752, before enclosure.

Source B

> They hang the man and flog the woman
> Who steals the goose from the common
> But leave the greater villain loose
> Who steals the common from the goose.

A popular rhyme of the period about enclosures.

Source C

There can be no question of the superior profit to the farmer of enclosures rather than open fields. In one case he is in chains; he can make no changes for the soil or prices, he is like a horse in a team, he must jog along with the rest.

John Middleton, an 18th-century writer, praising enclosures.

But enclosures also had good effects. They allowed the best farmers to use new methods like the **four-course rotation**. This involved using four fields, one each for wheat, barley or oats, clover, and turnips or swedes, swapping the crop round every year. None of the fields had to be left fallow, because the clover and root crops put back the nutrients which the grain crops had used up. Better still, the fields of clover and root crops could be used to graze animals. Their manure would enrich the soil. This meant more crops and bigger animals.

Farmers could also use bigger and better **tools** which would have been wasted on the strips. For example, **Jethro Tull** invented a **seed drill** and a **horse-drawn hoe**. The drill planted seeds evenly and prevented waste; the hoe weeded between the neat lines of crops.

Before enclosure, animals had mixed on the common land and bred freely. After enclosure, farmers could control breeding to get bigger animals with more meat or wool. **Robert Bakewell** developed a new breed of sheep called the **New Leicester** and the **Colling brothers** developed the **Durham shorthorn** cattle.

People like **Arthur Young** wrote books explaining the new farming methods. Farmers also gathered together to discuss them. **Thomas Coke** was a successful landowner who held gatherings for farmers on his land at Holkham. The **Duke of Bedford** did the same at Woburn.

These changes produced more food at reasonable prices. Most of the increase came from using more land. Between 1700 and 1820 Britain's wheat output almost doubled from 13 million quarters to 25 million. But there was also a gain in quality. The average weight of sheep and cattle at Smithfield Market in London more than doubled. The bigger landowners and tenant farmers made better profits and there was more work for labourers.

Source D

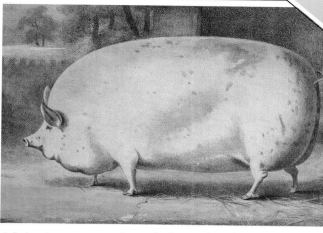

A Leicester sow, a product of selective breeding.

Source E

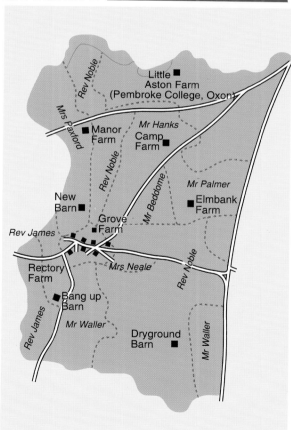

Aston Blank after enclosure. This map shows the new allocation of land.

The changes took place fastest in the 1790s and 1800s. From 1793 to 1815, Britain was at war with France. Imports of food were disrupted and prices rose rapidly. The price of wheat rose from an average of 50 shillings per quarter in 1790–4 to 102 shillings in 1810–14. This gave a huge incentive to farmers to enclose their land and introduce new methods

But after the war in 1815, wheat prices fell to 63 shillings. Farm profits fell and labourers' wages were cut. For almost 30 years most people on the land were in difficulties. It was a time of hardship for farmers and riots by labourers. This depression was only brought to an end by a new style of farming.

High farming

By the 1840s the growing population had started to force up the prices of food again and it was worth the farmers investing in **new methods**. Steam-driven reapers and threshers were brought in to save labour. Steam-driven pumps were used to get water off the land and stop crops rotting. Fowler's mole plough could lay clay drainage pipes under the soil for less than £5 per acre. **Fertilizers** were used to increase yields. Over 100,000 tons of guano (bird droppings rich in phosphates) were imported from Peru every year in the 1850s. Crushed bones, soot and chemicals made in Germany were also used. This extra use of machinery and scientific knowledge is called **high farming**.

No extra land was cultivated between 1840 and 1870. But production grew by 70 per cent, and farmers reduced their workforce by 300,000.

Source F

A cartoon published in 1830 showing the sorry state of 'Farmer Giles'. The letter says: 'This is to inform you that your children have been received into the workhouse.'

Source G

Steam-powered machinery for use on the farm, about 1850.

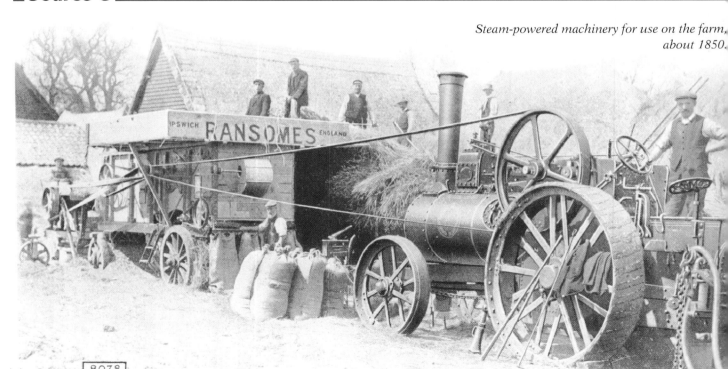

Source H

Unloading frozen meat imported from Australia.

Agricultural depression

But the golden age of farming came to an end in the 1870s. The following extract from the official **Agricultural Records** for the year 1879 explains why:

'August was very unfavourable. Pastures on clay land were as wet as in the middle of a normal winter. Grass was all trodden away and cattle sank to their knees. The quality of wheat and barley was wretched. No corn to sell and nobody cared to buy British produce. Vast quantities of grain pouring in from the USA. The first shipment of refrigerated beef arrived in Britain.'

This combination of a series of bad harvests at home and huge imports of grain and frozen meat from abroad sent British farming back into a **depression** which lasted until 1914. The whole structure of British agriculture changed. Thousands of grain farmers went bankrupt. They could not compete with the prices of American wheat grown on the prairies and transported to Britain by steam-driven trains and ships. Many of them switched to market gardening of vegetables and flowers. Some switched to dairy production too. Dairy farmers were not so badly off because they could use the cheap imported grain to feed their animals and because there was no foreign competition in fresh meat and milk.

British agriculture went through a series of sweeping changes between 1750 and 1914. They did not always happen at the same speed and they were not always progress. But they changed the face of farming.

Questions

Section A

1 The following diagram represents the use of fields in one year of the open field system. Copy it, then draw diagrams to show what would happen in the next two years.

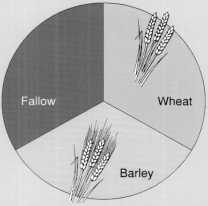

2 The following diagram represents the use of the fields in one year on an enclosed farm. Copy it, then draw diagrams to show what would happen in the next three years.

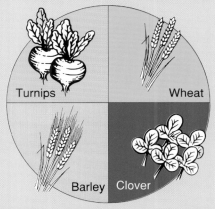

3 Extra wheat was grown during 1750–1815 mainly from farming more land. Explain two ways in which enclosures made more land available.

Section B

4 Re-read the last paragraph of the text on this page.
   a Describe five examples of things that changed in agriculture between 1750 and 1914.
   b Describe two things which **didn't** change.
   c Choose one change which was an improvement for some people in farming but not for others. Explain your answer.

6.2 Industrialization, 1750–1900

In 1750, most of Britain's seven million people lived in small rural villages. Farming was the main occupation. People were concerned mainly with growing enough food for their families to survive. Apart from London there were no cities and no factories. There was some industry scattered throughout the country. Woollen cloth, coal mining and iron making were the main industries.

Between 1750 and 1850 Britain became an **industrialized country**. The population grew rapidly during this period. There were 21 million people by 1851, and half of them lived in **huge cities**. Many of these cities were located on the coalfields of northern England and central Scotland. The most important industries were coal mining, iron and steel, cotton, wool and shipbuilding. Historians often call this change the **first Industrial Revolution**. Between 1850 and 1880 Britain was the world's leading industrial country and was sometimes called the **workshop of the world**. In 1851 the **Great Exhibition** was held in London with the idea of showing off Britain's industrial achievements to the world.

By 1880 the **United States** and **Germany** started to challenge Britain. They were soon to become the most powerful industrial countries in the world. By now newer, lighter industries were growing up: motor cars, bicycles, electrical engineering and chemicals. This was the **second Industrial Revolution**. Britain was slow to develop these new industries and continued to depend on the older industries to make money.

Source A

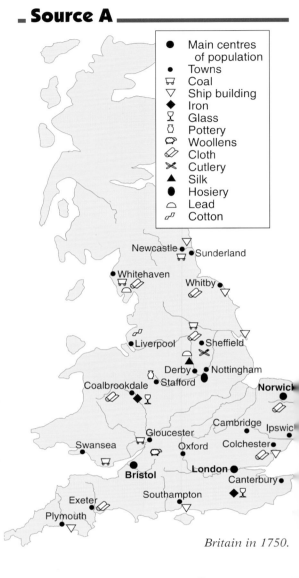

●	Main centres of population
•	Towns
⛏	Coal
▽	Ship building
◆	Iron
⚱	Glass
♗	Pottery
⬒	Woollens
⬟	Cloth
✕	Cutlery
▲	Silk
●	Hosiery
⌂	Lead
⬭	Cotton

Britain in 1750.

Source B

The South West Prospect of Manchester and Salford

Manchester and Salford in 1750.

Source C

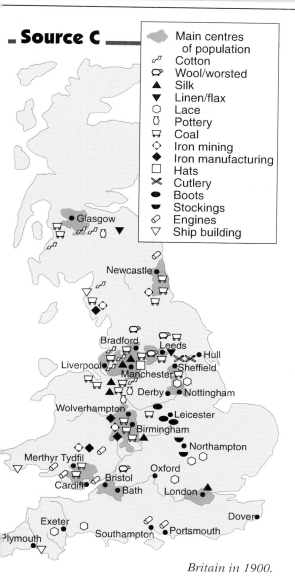

	Main centres of population
⌐	Cotton
⌐	Wool/worsted
▲	Silk
▼	Linen/flax
○	Lace
♡	Pottery
⊟	Coal
◇	Iron mining
◆	Iron manufacturing
☐	Hats
✕	Cutlery
●	Boots
⊽	Stockings
⊘	Engines
▽	Ship building

Britain in 1900.

Source D

Manchester in 1850.

Source E

	1750	1900
Cotton	2 million kilos	850 million kilos
Iron	40,000 tonnes	9 million tonnes
Coal	5 million tonnes	225 million tonnes
Steel	not known	5 million tonnes
Shipbuilding	50,000 tonnes	739,000 tonnes

Production figures for major industries, 1750–1900.

Source F

By the early 1830s nearly 250,000 workers were employed in textile factories, of whom one in eight were aged under 13. Bad ventilation led to diseases such as factory fever which was similar to typhus. Many factories had working days of fifteen hours or more. The long hours, often worked in cramped positions, sometimes led to permanent deformities. Factory owners imposed fines for lateness, talking at work or even opening a window.

From Robert Unwin, 'Britain since 1700', 1986.

Questions

Section A

1 Draw a **timeline** to show the years 1700–1900. Divide your line into the following sections:

- pre-industrial Britain
- the first Industrial Revolution
- the workshop of the world
- the second Industrial Revolution.

2 Describe the main features of each period.

Section B

3 a You have been asked to write a short account of the first Industrial Revolution for a history book. Write this using **either** Sources C and E, **or** Sources D and F.

b Compare your account with that of someone who used different sources. What do you notice?

c How can you explain the differences?

d Would your account have differed if you had been allowed to use all the sources? Explain your answer.

4 The word **revolution** means complete and sometimes violent change. Do you think the phrase **Industrial Revolution** is a good one to describe the changes in Britain between 1750 and 1900? Explain your answer.

5 Was the industrialization of Britain between 1750 and 1900 **progress**? Explain your answer.

6.3 The Textile Industry

In the early 18th century the making of **woollen cloth** was the most important industry in Britain. Like most other industries it was based on the **domestic system** – the workers produced the cloth in their own homes. When the cloth was ready it was collected by the **master clothier** and sold at the nearest market town.

When the population began to grow quickly after 1750, there was a need for more cloth to be produced. The domestic system could not cope with this demand, as the hand-worked spinning wheels and looms were too slow. This led people to invent a series of **new machines** which were much quicker and able to produce far more cloth. These machines were introduced first into the **cotton textile** industry of Lancashire and central Scotland.

People liked cotton fabrics because they were light and easy to wash. Wool was a much older industry; most people in the woollen industry were against the introduction of new machines to begin with. The Yorkshire woollen industry did not become mechanized until 30 years after machines were introduced into the cotton industry. As a result, wool lost its position as the leading textile industry.

One of the new spinning machines, Richard Arkwright's **water frame**, marked an especially important change. It was too big to be used in the home and needed water to power it. From this point onwards spinning was usually done in **mills** (factories) built by the sides of fast-flowing streams. When the **steam engine** was perfected it was able to drive all sorts of machinery, so the textile factories were then built near to the coalfields.

Weaving took longer than spinning to become factory-based in both the cotton and the woollen industry. During this time the domestic **hand-loom weavers** had plenty of thread to weave. They became very prosperous and were reluctant to give up their trade. Eventually, however, the success of the **power loom** meant that they too were forced to become factory workers.

By 1870 all the processes in the various textile industries had become fully mechanized. In 1880 cotton cloth made up one-third of Britain's total exports.

Questions

Section A

1 Draw a timeline showing the main changes in the textile industry.

2 Describe the domestic system as seen in Source A.

3 Describe the factory system as seen in Source C.

4 How realistic do you think Sources A and C are? Give reasons for your answer.

Section B

5 Copy and complete the following table summarizing the main changes in the textile industry between 1750 and 1850.

	Power	Location	Output	Market
1750 - domestic system				
1850 - factory system				

6 Did the factory system introduce child labour?

7 'Changes in the textile industry happened at the same pace everywhere and affected everybody in the same way'. Explain why you agree or disagree with this statement.

Inventions in the textile industry

Year	Inventor	Machine	Process	Location
1733	John Kay	Flying shuttle	Weaving	House
1764	James Hargreaves	Spinning Jenny	Spinning	House
1769	Richard Arkwright	Water frame	Spinning	Factory
1779	Samuel Crompton	Mule	Spinning	Factory
1785	Edmund Cartwright	Power loom	Weaving	Factory

Source A

The domestic system in the late 18th century.

Source B

Area	1787	1835
Cheshire	8	109
Derbys	22	96
Lancs	41	683
Yorks	11	126
Scotland	19	159
(Total in Britain	**143**	**1,263)**

Number of cotton factories in selected areas of Britain, 1787 and 1835. From R. Burn, 'Statistics of the Cotton Trade', 1847.

Source C

A spinning factory in 1830.

6.4 Coal Mining

From about 1750 onwards there was an increased **demand** for **coal**. Wood had become scarce, and people were using coal to heat their homes. Coal was also being used as the main fuel in **iron making**, **brick making**, **brewing** and **soap boiling**. More industries were using **steam power**, and this required vast amounts of coal. Soon all the coal near the surface had been used up, and miners had to dig deep **vertical shaft mines**. By 1830 some mines were over 300 metres deep.

Deep shaft mining was not easy. The deeper the mines were, the greater the dangers. These included **flooding**, **choke-damp** and **fire-damp**. Moving the coal up the shaft to the surface was also very difficult. The information box below tells you how a number of inventions tried to solve these problems.

The problems of shaft mining

Problem	Methods tried to overcome the problem
Choke-damp (foul air)	**Exhaust fans** to suck foul air from the mines
Fire-damp (methane)	Gas would explode if it came into contact with a naked flame; the **safety lamp** was invented in 1815 to combat the problem
Flooding	**Steam pumps** were used to drain away water
Hauling coal up the shaft	To begin with, coal was carried up ladders; by 1840 **steel cables** and **steam haulage** were coming into use

Source A

In 1815 Sir Humphry Davy invented a safety lamp. A miner could now work away, knowing his light would not cause an explosion.

From P. F. Speed, 'History through Maps and Diagrams: The Industrial Revolution to the Present Day', 1985.

Source B

Though the use of safety lamps did not put an end to the risk of explosions, their number was greatly reduced.

From R. N. Rundle, 'Britain's Economic and Social Development', 1973.

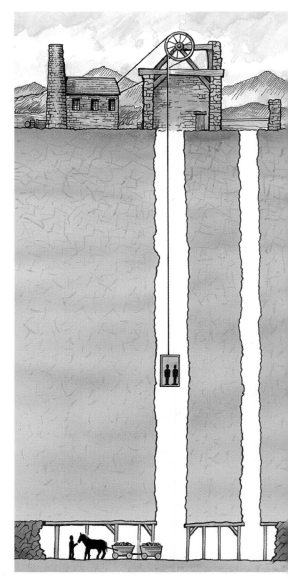

A vertical shaft mine in about 1800.

Source C

THE SECOND EXPLOSION AT THE OAKS COLLIERY, BARNSLEY.—SEE PRECEDING PAGE.

An explosion at Oaks Colliery, Barnsley, on 12 December 1866. Three hundred and fifty miners died. This engraving was used to illustrate a news report at the time.

Source E

Many of the changes were introduced only towards the middle of the 19th century, and many districts remained backward. While the new forms of ventilation were in general use, along with steam pumps in the north of England by 1850, they were slow to be adopted in other coalfields such as South Staffordshire, South Wales and Scotland.

From Neil Buxton, 'The Economic Development of the British Coal Industry', 1978.

Source D

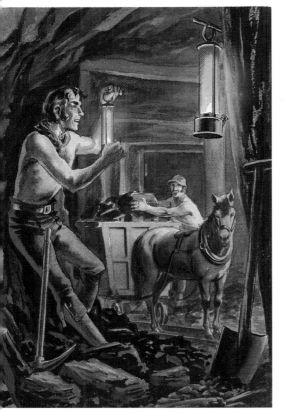

An artist's impression of coal mining after the invention of the safety lamp. This painting was made in 1961.

Questions

Section A

1 Why did the demand for coal increase?

2 If shaft mining was so dangerous, why do you think people were willing to do it? Explain your answer.

3 What improvements were made in the way coal was mined in the 19th century?

Section B

4 How does Source A differ from Source B?

5 a What impression does Source D give of coal mining?
  b Do you think this is an accurate interpretation of coal mining in the 19th century? Explain your answer.

6 Many school history textbooks lead us to think that the new methods of coal mining were introduced very quickly and in every coal mine in Britain.
  a How does Source E differ in its interpretation?
  b Why do you think it differs?
  c How could the viewpoint in Source E be checked?

6.5 Iron and Steel

In 1700 the **iron industry** was in trouble. Wood, used for making charcoal to fire the **blast furnaces**, was fast running out. A new fuel was desperately needed to **smelt** iron ore.

In 1709 **Abraham Darby I**, of Coalbrookdale, found that if coal was first turned into **coke** it could be used to smelt iron ore. But Darby kept his discovery a secret. It wasn't until after 1760 that his new method came into more general use. Even then, Darby's method only produced **pig iron** that was suitable for **casting**.

The best-quality iron (**wrought iron**) was still difficult to make. Pig iron had to be reheated and hammered to remove the impurities. It took twelve hours to convert one tonne of pig iron into wrought iron. In 1783 **Henry Cort** devised the **puddling process**. This was a method for rapidly producing lots of wrought iron. The wrought iron could be taken, semi-molten, to the **rolling mill**, where it was shaped into pipes, bars, girders and sheet iron.

This led to **ironworks** being built near to supplies of coal. The works also became much bigger, with blast furnaces, foundries and forges all on the same site. These improvements in iron making helped the Industrial Revolution to take place. Iron was a vital product, used to make machinery, steam engines, rails, bridges, ships and locomotives. British iron was **exported** all over world.

Cheap steel arrives

Steel is an even better metal than wrought iron. Until the 1850s, however, it was only possible to produce it in small amounts. In 1856 **Henry Bessemer** invented a converter which speedily turned liquid iron into steel. Then, in 1879 **Sidney Gilchrist Thomas** and **Percy Gilchrist** invented the **basic process**. This allowed steel to be made very quickly in large amounts using poor-quality iron ore. This was a major breakthrough.

The **United States** and **Germany** had huge amounts of poor-quality iron ore that they previously could not use. Now both countries became giant steel producers. Although Middlesborough grew into a large steel-producing town, Britain was unable to produce as much as its two rivals. Britain's steel production increased from 2 million tonnes in 1880 to 7 million tonnes in 1914. In the same period the USA's production went up from 1.5 million tonnes to 31 million tonnes! Steel replaced wrought iron as the main building material. The **Eiffel Tower** (1889) and the **Forth Railway Bridge** (1890) were both made of steel.

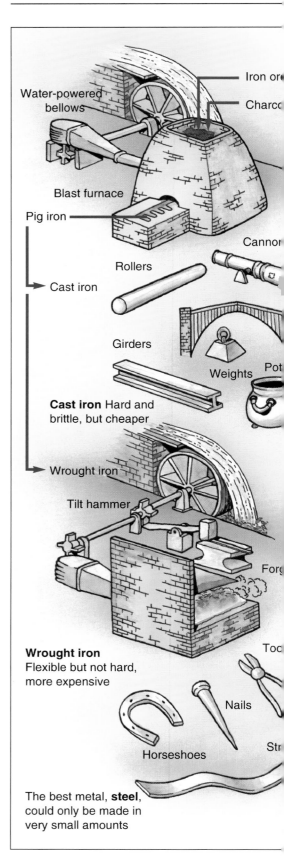

Water-powered bellows

Iron ore

Charco

Blast furnace

Pig iron

Cast iron

Rollers

Cannon

Girders

Weights   Pot

Cast iron Hard and brittle, but cheaper

Wrought iron

Tilt hammer

Forg

Wrought iron
Flexible but not hard, more expensive

Too

Nails

Horseshoes

Str

The best metal, **steel**, could only be made in very small amounts

How iron was made in 1700.

Source A

The world's first iron bridge, opened in 1781, built across the River Severn by Abraham Darby III. Some people were against using iron and wanted the bridge to be built of wood or stone.

Source B

The Forth Railway Bridge, built of steel and opened in 1890.

Source C

Year	Iron produced in Britain (tonnes)
1720	25,000
1788	70,000
1820	450,000
1850	2,000,000

Iron production in Britain, 1720–1850.

Source D

Lymington Ironworks, Northumbria, 1835.

Questions

Section A

1 Show the developments in the iron and steel industry on a timeline.

2 Study Source D. Does this suggest that ironworks would be very expensive to set up?

3 Compare Source A with Source B. Is this an example of progress? Explain your answer.

Section B

4 a Each of the following factors might be a **cause** of the discovery of new methods of making iron in the 18th century. Copy out each factor and say whether it was a cause or not. Explain your answers.
   ● A quickly growing population.
   ● A shortage of wood.
   ● Brilliant individuals.
   ● Large supplies of coal.
   ● The growth of the textile industries.
   ● The invention of the steam engine.
   b Which of the causes was the most important? Give reasons for your answer.

5 What were the results of the new methods of making iron?

6 What were the short-term and long-term consequences of the basic process?

6.6 The Age of Steam

Early forms of power

In 1700 **power** was provided by **human muscles**, **animals** (horses, mules and oxen), **water mills** and **windmills**. During the 18th century a much more reliable form of power was perfected: the **steam engine**.

As early as 1698 **Thomas Savery** had built a steam engine to drain water from tin-mines in Cornwall. It was a rather clumsy machine but it set an example for other inventors to follow. Between 1705 and 1712 **Thomas Newcomen** of Dartmouth built a steam engine to pump water from mines. It was a better machine than Savery's, and by 1775 over 100 of the machines were at work in coal mines in Northumbria. But Newcomen's engine used huge amounts of coal and could only be used for pumping water.

Enter James Watt

In 1763 **James Watt** (1736–1819), a maker of scientific instruments at Glasgow University, was asked to repair a model of a Newcomen engine. His sharp mind soon picked up a number of design faults, and he thought he might be able to build a better steam engine. Watt did not have any money and he needed a financial backer. He was able to win the support of **Dr John Roebuck**, the owner of the Carron Ironworks in Scotland. Watt made good progress and managed to design a more effective engine than Newcomen's. But in 1773 Roebuck went bankrupt – Watt was left without any money. Was all his good work to be lost?

The limitations of early methods of power.

Matthew Boulton, the owner of the Soho Hardware works in Birmingham, heard of his problem. He told Watt he would provide him with money if he moved to Birmingham. In 1774 Watt moved south. He immediately struck up a good relationship with **William Murdoch**, Boulton's foreman. Together, in 1781, they invented a **rotary motion** steam engine. This engine was an amazing breakthrough – it could be used to **drive** many different machines and was not just limited to draining mines.

Boulton now took a big gamble by borrowing £17,000 from the bank to put the new engine into production. His boldness paid off. By 1800 there were over 500 Boulton and Watt engines at work in different factories across the country. The engines were used, for example, in textile mills, breweries, iron foundries and flour mills.

Watt's engines needed accurately made parts in order to work properly. This led to the growth of the **machine tool** industry. In the 19th century **high-pressure** rotary motion steam engines were being used to power railway locomotives and steamships.

Electricity

In the 1880s **Thomas Edison** built the world's first **power station** for generating and distributing electricity. American and German factories were quick to use this cleaner form of power. British industry, however, was slow to change to electricity and continued to rely on steam power until well into the 20th century.

Questions

Section A

1 What early forms of power were available in 1700? Why were they unreliable?

2 Draw a **timeline**, starting in 1698, showing the main events in the invention of the steam engine.

3 Look at Source A. How was the energy produced by the engine transferred to the machines?

Section B

4 Perhaps **chance** was the most important reason why Watt was able to invent the rotary motion steam engine. Explain why.

5 What were the **consequences** of Watt's invention of the rotary motion steam engine?

6 Were the changes in coal mining and iron making, and the invention of the steam engine, **all** needed for the Industrial Revolution to happen? Explain your answer.

Source A

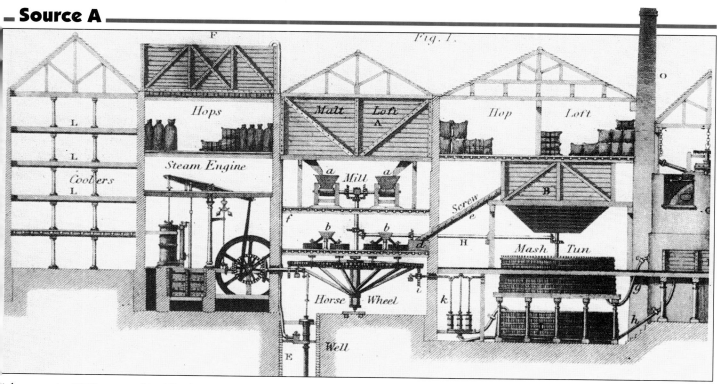

A brewery in 1819 powered by Watt's rotary motion steam engine. This one engine drove all the machines in the factory.

6.7 Road Transport

Most people and goods in the 18th century were transported by road on **horses**, **pack-horses**, **carts** or **stage-coaches**. Yet a survey of the roads in 1750 would have shown that they were in very poor condition (see Source A). Outside towns, they were usually just tracks created by regular use. They were muddy in winter and heavily rutted in summer. Since 1555 the law had said that the rich people in each parish had to pay for tools and materials to repair the roads. Every year poorer people had to do six days of unpaid work on the roads. But this system did not produce good enough roads.

Turnpike trusts

Industry needed better roads. It needed to get raw materials – like coal, iron ore and wool – to the workshops and factories. It needed to get finished goods – like cloth – to its markets. These were heavy and bulky goods to transport. Factory owners were prepared to pay for better roads.

Some people set up groups to run stretches of road like a business. An Act of Parliament gave them permission to charge fees to all the travellers who used the road. In return, they would use some of this money to pay for road repairs and improvements. These groups were called **turnpike trusts**.

Some people disliked paying fees on roads that they had used before for free. But in most places the turnpikes were a success (see Source B). Eight turnpike trusts were set up between 1700 and 1750 and 55 between 1750 and 1800. By 1830, 1,000 trusts controlled 23,000 miles of road, about one-sixth of Britain's total.

The turnpike trusts employed expert road builders to repair or replace the old roads. The most famous of the time were **John Metcalfe**, **Thomas Telford** and **John Macadam**.

From about 1810 better roads brought a boom in **stage coach travel**. A journey from London to York, which took five days in 1750, took only one day by 1840. Coaching inns sprang up along the routes to provide food and fresh horses. From 1784 these coaches carried the **Royal Mail**. By 1840 there were 23,000 people employed by the turnpike trusts and over 30,000 employed by the coaching companies.

But the 'golden age of coaching' came to an end in the 1840s. **Canals** could take goods more cheaply. **Railways** could take passengers more quickly. Horse-drawn transport only survived for

Source A

I know not words sufficient to describe this damned road. You will meet there with ruts that I actually measured four feet deep and floating with mud after a wet summer. What can it be like after winter?

From Arthur Young, 'A Tour through the North of England', 1771.

Source B

Turnpikes have been set up on several great roads at which all carriages, droves of cattle and travellers on horseback are obliged to pay an easy toll; that is to say, a horse a penny, a coach three pence, a cart four pence, a waggon six pence. But in no place is it thought to be a burden that I ever met with, the benefit of a good road making amends for that little charge.

Daniel Defoe, an 18th-century traveller and writer, gives his opinion of the turnpikes.

Source C

A toll house, built in the late 18th century, by the side of a modern road. It was built by a turnpike trust to collect tolls.

Source D

A toll house from a 19th century print.

short-distance work, for example in the towns. Some people tried to bring steam power on to the roads (see Source E), but the heavy steam carriages were not practical.

Road transport only revived when **petrol-driven cars** became common. The first motor car was built in Germany by Gottlieb Daimler in 1883. There were 10,000 on the roads of Britain by 1905. But that's a story for the 20th century.

Source E

The London to Bath steam coach passing a coaching inn.

Questions

Section A

1 Copy out the following paragraph, choosing the best alternative from the words in *italics*.
Turnpikes were set up to *improve roads/run stagecoaches*. Most were set up between *1750 and 1800/1800 and 1830*. Road transport became less important because *railways/canals* were cheaper and *railways/canals* were faster.

2 Do you think the road described in Source A was a turnpike?

3 How might you find the routes of old turnpikes that ran through your area?

4 Steam coaches were not a success.
   a Can you suggest why?
   b Does this mean that there is no point in historians studying them?

Section B

5 What changes took place in road transport between 1700 and 1900?

6 Draw a **graph** showing the **rate** of change in road transport between 1700 and 1900. The line on your graph should go up when road transport was improving, down when it was getting worse, and straight when there was no change. Show your graph to other people and explain it.

7 What does the shape of your graph tell you about change in history?

6.8 Water Transport

Before Britain's roads were improved, it was sometimes better to travel by **river** or by **sea**. Coal from north-east England usually came to London by sea. Boats were quicker and could take heavier loads. Goods could be carried all the way from London to Oxford by barge along the River Thames. But rivers were usually not straight, could be too shallow in summer and flooded or frozen in winter; bridges and fords blocked traffic.

Canals

In 1757 a canal called the **Sankey Brook Navigation** was opened. It linked St Helens to the River Mersey and was paid for by local businessmen. In 1761 the **Bridgewater Canal**, from Worsley to Manchester, was built by **James Brindley**. The cost of this ten-mile canal was £20,000, paid by the **Duke of Bridgewater**. The duke owned a coal mine at Worsley and wanted to reduce the cost of taking his coal to Manchester. By 1765 he halved the price of his coal and still made a profit. He also charged other traders to use the canal. He was soon making £80,000 per year in fees.

▬ Source A ▬

▬ Source B ▬

Liverpool and Northwich have generally been supplied with coal from Prescot and Whitson. Such coal hath become scarce, as well as the advanced price due to the rate of carriage, much to the harm of trade and factories.

A report by Liverpool Council in 1754 when it was planning for the Sankey Brook Navigation.

▬ Source C ▬

The most obvious effect of the new canal is that, for manufacturers, it cuts the cost of sending goods and opens up a way to the sea. It increases the number of factories in places where the land was of little value. It also helps merchants export greater quantities of goods and it helps those parts that lie a long way from the sea.

Josiah Wedgwood, an 18th-century businessman, describing the Grand Trunk Canal.

▬ Source D ▬

The staple goods of Manchester, Birmingham and Wolverhampton – cheese, salt, lime, stone, timber, corn, paper and bricks – are carried along the canal to the people of London. In return, groceries, cotton, tin, manure and raw materials constantly pass to the manufacturing districts.

A writer describing the Grand Trunk Canal in the 1790s.

A lock on the Regent's Canal in 1827. Canals need to have water that is level, so that barges can move easily both ways. If the canal is on sloping land, locks are used to separate the lower stretch of the canal from the higher one. Barges wanting to go up a slope are floated into the lock and the set of lock gates closed behind them. Water is then allowed to flow into the lock from the higher stretch of canal, and the barge is raised. The lock gates in front of the barge are opened; the barge is then floated out the other side.

Source E

A contemporary painting of the launch of the Great Britain.

Other businessmen employed engineers like Brindley, **Thomas Telford** and **William Jessop** to build canals. Brindley's most famous is the **Grand Trunk Canal**, which links the Rivers Trent and Mersey. By 1790 there was a network linking the four major ports of Bristol, Liverpool, Hull and London. During the 1790s, 50 more canals were built.

By the 1840s the **railways** brought the end of the canal era. Rail could carry goods much faster and more cheaply. But other types of transport on water were booming.

In 1845, the *Rainbow*, the first **clipper** – a new design of fast wooden sailing ships – was built. These clippers began to cross the oceans of the world at record speeds. **Steam-powered ships** were also being tried. In 1838 two new steamships, the *Sirius* (an American ship) and the *Great Western* (a wooden paddle-steamer built by **Isambard Kingdom Brunel**), both crossed the Atlantic. Then came **iron ships**. Brunel's next ship, the *Great Britain*, was launched in 1843. It ran aground off Ireland in 1846 but didn't break up because of its iron hull. By 1881 the *Servia* became the world's first ocean-going **steel ship.** It was built in Scotland and could carry 1,250 passengers.

Questions

Section A

1 Read the last paragraph on this page. Make a table with headings and columns. Put into your table all of the important information from the paragraph.

Section B

2 Why do you think the businessmen of St Helens paid for the Sankey Brook Navigation?

3 What were the consequences for the Duke of Bridgewater of building the Bridgewater Canal?

4 What were the consequences of canals for Britain? Try to divide your answer into different kinds of effects and to assess how important each one was.

6.9 The Railways

Rails had long been used to carry heavy vehicles. For example, tracks called **waggonways** were used in the mines of the north-east of England to carry carts loaded with coal. But they were horse-drawn. In 1804 **Richard Trevithick** built a **locomotive** – a steam engine which moved along wheels on rails. This was the first railway engine, but it was unreliable. Trevithick only built it to demonstrate his invention on a circular track. Other people tried to improve on his design. **William Hedley** built the **Puffing Billy** in 1813 to use on the waggonways of Wylam Colliery. By 1823 there were 20 locomotives on the waggonways of the north-east.

Then there was a breakthrough. The mine-owners in Durham decided to build a railway from **Stockton** to **Darlington,** to get the coal out of the South Durham coalfield more easily. They employed **George Stephenson** to build it, and he persuaded them to let him build it for steam locomotives. In September 1825 the line was opened with two engines, 'Locomotive No. 1' and 'Experiment', coupled together to pull 21 coal waggons 25 miles at 8 miles per hour. The line was soon making a profit.

In 1830 a railway opened running from **Liverpool to Manchester.** This was intended to carry mostly freight (goods). By 1850 it was carrying up to 200,000 passengers per week at over 40 miles per hour.

Railway mania

Between 1825 and 1835 Parliament agreed to the building of 54 new railways. Not everyone was keen. Some people complained about the pollution; others said the noise upset farm animals; some towns, like Northampton and Oxford, refused to let the railways in for several years. But at times there was so much activity that people called it '**railway mania**'. There were 39 new lines agreed in 1836–7. In 1846 alone, a further 5,000 miles were started. By 1900 Britain had 22,000 miles of track.

Source B

She goes along wheels which are her feet and are moved by bright steel legs called pistons; the reins, bit and bridle of this wonderful beast are a small steel handle which a small child could manage. I feel rather inclined to pat this snorting little animal.

Fanny Kemble, a 19th-century actress, describing her first view of a train.

Source C

A cartoon with the title 'The Effects of the Railroad on Brute Creation', 1831. 'Brute creation' refers to the animals in the cartoon.

Source A

First-class travel on the Liverpool to Manchester line, 1831.

The railways helped **industry**; they made it cheaper to carry raw materials and finished products. Manufacturers could sell cheaper goods and still make more profit. Railways also bought from industry – iron for rails and locomotives, coal for fuel, and bricks for embankments and stations. Only the coaching and canal companies suffered.

Farmers now got their produce to market more cheaply and could send it further and faster. This was important for perishable produce like milk, fruit and flowers.

The railways also provided **jobs**. Twenty thousand people were employed to build the London to Birmingham line. In 1854 there were 90,000 jobs in railway maintenance. Whole new towns emerged. **Crewe** grew from a village of 203 people in 1841 into a railway depot with a population of 18,000 in 1871.

The public didn't only get cheaper food and goods and more work. The **mail** became quicker; **national newspapers** started up; **travel** became easier. **Holidays** in seaside towns like Brighton became possible.

Before long, the hundreds of railway companies that had started out began to **combine**. By 1900 eleven companies shared all the lines in the country. In 1948 the railways were **nationalized** and are all now run by one company.

Source D

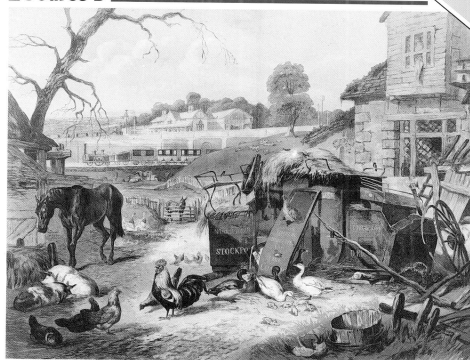

Another view of the effects of the railways, from about 1840.

Questions

Section A

1 What were the **intended** effects of railways?

2 What were the **unintended** effects?

Section B

3 Study Sources A, B and E. Are they in favour of the railways?

4 Look at Source C. It is obviously criticizing the railways. Explain how.

5 Look at Source D. Is this just a pretty rural scene? Or is there a hidden message here?

6 What do the sources in this unit tell us about the railways?

Source E

Third-class travel on the Liverpool to Manchester line, 1840s.

7.1 Working Conditions

When people began to build the first **factories**, there were very few **regulations** about **working conditions**. Some employers took advantage of this. There were complaints about long hours and low wages; but there always had been. There were also concerns about child labour, although children had always helped their parents in workshops and the fields. The main new concerns were the **dangers to health** in the factories and mines; **noise**, **heat**, **overcrowding**, and the **exploitation** of women and children.

Women were usually paid half and children a third of a man's wage. So many employers were tempted to use women and children to do work more suited to full-grown men. Another complaint was the loss of independence. The factory bell and the relentless machines now ruled the lives of workers who had been used to controlling their own hours and methods of work.

Source A

Workers in a textile mill, about 1840.

Source B

My hours of work at Mr Connell's mill were from a few minutes before half-past five in the morning till seven at night. Half an hour for breakfast. An hour for dinner. No baggin [tea].

A factory worker quoted in 'The report of a Royal Commission to Parliament', 1833.

Source C

In this trade [fork grinding], 855 perish out of every 1,000 between 20 and 40 years of age, while in England the average is only 296.

From the 'Medical Times', 1843.

Source D

In Willenhall, the children are shamefully and most cruelly beaten with a horsewhip, strap, stick, hammer, handle, file or whatever tool is nearest to hand, or are struck with the clenched fist or kicked.

From 'The Report of the Children's Employment Commission', 1843.

Source E

The youngest children in the mines are called trappers. Their job consists of sitting in a little hole by each door in the mine shafts. There they sit, with a string attached to the door, and pull it the moment they hear the carts at hand. They sit in the dark all the time the pit is worked.

From 'The Report on the Working Conditions in the Mines', 1842.

Source F

The racking noise of engines, the hell of sounds; the dragging, wearying monotony of the machine; the stifling heat; the unbroken noise; the need for constant action on the part of the workers – these render the place and the employment all but intolerable.

Douglas Jerrold, a journalist, writing in 1840.

Source G

Underground in a Staffordshire mine, 1860.

Source H

Little boys and girls are seen here at work at the tip-punching machines with their fingers in constant danger of being punched off. 'They seldom lose the hand,' said one of the owners, 'it only takes off a finger at the first or second joint. Sheer carelessness.'

From 'The Third Report of the Children's Employment Commission', 1864.

Source I

The factory folk are better clothed, better fed and better conducted than many other classes of working people. I found the mill a large building and very clean. The working rooms are spacious, well ventilated and lofty, kept at an even temperature and exceedingly clean. I observed great care in the boxing up of dangerous machinery and was told that accidents were very rare.

A visitor to a mill in Bolton in 1844, reported in Chambers' Journal'.

Questions

Section A

1 Describe the hardships of working conditions in factories, workshops and mines in the mid-19th century. Organize your work under these headings:
  ● long hours
  ● harsh discipline
  ● dangerous machinery
  ● exploitation of women and children
  ● monotony and lack of independence.
  Refer to all the sources in this unit to support your description.

Section B

2 Which are the more useful sources to historians: picture sources or written sources? Give reasons for your answer.

3 Source I seems to give a different impression of working conditions than the other sources. Does this mean:
  a Source I is right and all the others are wrong or exaggerated?
  b Source I is wrong?
  c something else?
  Explain your answer.

4 Several of the sources in this unit are from official government inquiries. Do you think that they are more reliable than the other sources here? Explain your answer.

7.2 Factory Reform

Governments were not keen to control working conditions at first. They felt that restricting the freedom of employers would cut their **profits.** Even some working people said that they didn't want laws that reduced hours or child labour because this could cause more **poverty.** Another key idea which slowed down new laws was **laissez faire:** the idea that there were some areas of life in which the government should not interfere. Working conditions were a private arrangement between a person and his or her employer; they were no business of the government.

But gradually governments realized that they had to act. The normal pattern was that **pressure groups** would start campaigns for new laws. Then the government would have to set up an **inquiry** to investigate what all the fuss was about. Then, when the inquiry published an **official report**, the government had to do something about it.

The first campaigners were humanitarian factory owners like **Robert Owen** and **John Fielden.** After a while, they began to press for a maximum ten-hour working day and became known as the **ten-hour movement.** Some MPs, like **Michael Sadler**, took up the issue. But perhaps the most famous and most effective campaigner was **Lord Anthony Ashley Cooper** (later **Earl of Shaftesbury**). He was one of a group of evangelical Christians who campaigned against the evils of society.

Gradually, Parliament protected workers, especially children, in more and more industries. It also appointed **inspectors** to enforce the law.

1819 Factory Act

Applied only to cotton mills. Banned employment of children under 9 years old. Set maximum of 72-hour week for children aged 9–16, with $1\frac{1}{2}$ hours for meal breaks.

1833 Althorp's Factory Act

Applied to all textile industries. Banned work for children under 9 years old. Set maximum of 42-hour week for children aged 9–13 and 69 hours for those aged 13–16. Night work banned for those under 18. Children not to clean machinery in motion. Factory inspectors appointed to enforce the laws. (Only four at first, but it was a start.)

1842 Mines and Collieries Act

Applied only to mines. Banned underground work for women and children under 10 years old. No winding gear to be operated by those under 15. Mine inspectors appointed.

1844 Graham's Factory Act

Applied to all textile factories. Reduced minimum age of work to 8 years old, but set maximum hours of $6\frac{1}{2}$ hours per day for those aged 8–13 and 12 hours for those under 18 and all women. All dangerous machinery to be fenced in.

1847 Fielden's Factory Act

Maximum 10-hour day for those under 18 and women.

1867 Factories and Workshops Act

Applied all previous laws on working conditions to all factories and workshops with more than 50 workers.

1874 Factories and Workshops Act

Maximum $56\frac{1}{2}$-hour week for all factory workers. This meant a 10-hour day Mondays to Fridays and $6\frac{1}{2}$ hours on Saturdays.

1878 Factory Act

Applied all previous laws and all inspectors to every workplace with machinery, so all workers in industry protected.

Source A

A 19th-century factory inspector checking the ages of child workers.

Source E

Extreme hardship would be inflicted upon tens of thousands of families in Lancashire and Yorkshire by a law fixing the hours at eight or even ten hours and absolutely forbidding the employment of a child for a minute longer.

From the 'Leeds Mercury', December 1831.

Questions

Section A

1 Explain why many people were against laws to control working conditions. Refer to Sources B–E in your answer.

2 Do you think the artist who drew Source A approved of the factory laws? Explain your answer.

Section B

3 Which of the changes brought about by the new laws controlling working conditions do you think was most important? Explain your answer.

4 Consider these three types of changes which the new laws brought in:
 a limited hours of work.
 b safety regulations.
 c factory and mines inspectors.
 Are these changes all separate, or are they connected in any way?

5 Did working conditions change for everyone equally as a result of the new laws?

Source B

Our only advantages are in cheap machinery and low rates of interest. By restricting mills, we give up these advantages and hand them over to the enemy.

From Robert Hyde Greg, 'The Factory Questions Considered', 1837.

Source C

In a mill, the whole net profit is derived from the work produced in the last hour of the day. If the hours of work were reduced by one hour per day, the whole profit would be destroyed.

Nassau Senior, an economist, giving his opinion in 1837.

Source D

The 1833 Factory Act is dictated by the best of intentions. But it is a crude piece of legislation calculated to harass [trouble] the manufacturers by minute interference, while it secures for the children more leisure and less wages than their parents will approve.

From the 'Leeds Mercury', August 1833.

7.3 Poverty

Since the 16th century, poorer people who were unable to support themselves had been able to turn to the parish magistrates for **poor relief**. They were called **paupers**. They could be on low wages or unemployed; they might be orphaned children or sick. The type of help they got varied from parish to parish. It also depended on the reason why they were poor. The help could be a place in the workhouse, work in the fields, an apprenticeship with a local craftsman, or even money. In 1795 the parish of **Speenhamland** in Berkshire had worked out a system which gave people money depending on their wages and the price of bread.

By about 1830 the **poor laws** needed to be reformed. They were very expensive, and they varied too much from place to place. Ratepayers said that the Speenhamland system made people lazy and encouraged them to rely on help from the parish. Workers said it encouraged employers to pay low wages, and so degraded people by forcing them to ask for help through no fault of their own. In 1830 there were riots over the south of England, called the **Swing Riots**. Some people thought the Speenhamland system was to blame.

In 1834 the **Poor Law Amendment Act** was passed. The Act was largely the work of **Edwin Chadwick**. It said that magistrates should try to abolish all poor relief except the **workhouse**. Workhouses had to be a last resort for the poor – so they were made 'less eligible' (less desirable) than the worst conditions outside the workhouse.

The amended law became known as the **New Poor Law**. It remained in force for the rest of the century, though it was not always possible to enforce it fully.

Source A

> The New Poor Law is working very satisfactorily; the great body of the labouring poor have become reconciled to it; the workhouse is held in great dread; there is greater seeking for employment.

Comment by the chairman of the Board of Governors, Market Harborough, 1836.

Source B

> I consider that, for industry, cleanliness and good order, this house cannot be exceeded, with the healthy appearance of men, women and children.

Dr L. T. Nayle reporting on a visit to the Andover workhouse in about 1840.

Source C

An illustration from 'Jessie Phillips', a novel published in 1844. A woman asking for relief has fainted at the news that she will have to go into the workhouse.

Source D

Financially, the New Poor Law was a success. In 1831 nearly £7 million had been spent on the poor rates. In 1851 this sum had fallen to below £5 million, in spite of a rise of 29 per cent in the population. The numbers of paupers had also fallen.

From John Patrick, 'Waterloo to the Great Exhibition', 1981.

Source E

The commissioners were not trying deliberately to be cruel. For example, they said that no boy should be beaten by anyone but the the master of the workhouse; and that no girl should ever be beaten. Most workhouses provided a better standard of living than a labourer would have in his own cottage and the food was better. Much of the food was cheap – potato, bread or suet pudding – but they would have meat three to four times per week and cheese for breakfast or supper for protein. The amounts of food were quite large.

It was not living conditions which made paupers hate and fear the workhouse; it was that the inmate lost his or her sense of identity.

From Susan J. Styles, 'The Poor Law', 1985.

Source F

Then there was the dreaded workhouse. It was the economical policy of the Poor Law Commissioners to make workhouses so detestable and brutal that the poor might be tempted to commit suicide rather than 'go on the parish'. It amounted to the same thing in the end. Throughout the Victorian era, workhouses remained a scandal.

From Nicholas Bentley, 'The Victorian Scene 1837–1901', 1968.

Source G

Most paupers were sick, mentally ill, orphaned or widowed. Able-bodied men and women were a minority. Yet to deal with the minority, pauperism was made something to be ashamed of.

The workhouses were a complete disgrace. The government report had suggested different workhouses for different groups of paupers. The Act resulted in single workhouses for all the paupers in the union. There was no separate provision for the sick or the mentally ill. And a common dining room and chapel brought together several times a day all the inmates, from the idiot to the young child and expectant mother.

The prospect of the workhouse was humiliating to northern industrial workers who fell on hard times because of economic depression. It was these workers who provided the raw material for what was almost a revolution in the north of England in the 1830s and 1840s.

Source H

| 1830–4 | £6.75 million |
| 1835–9 | £4.5 million |

Statistics showing the average cost of the Poor Law.

Source I

If I am ever confined to one of those hellish Poor Law Bastilles, and my wife be torn from me, because I am poor, I will burn the whole pile down to the ground.

Richard Oastler, a northerner who campaigned against the Poor Law, giving his view in 1835.

Questions

Section A

1 Which of the sources in this unit are **primary** and which are **secondary**? Explain your answer.

Section B

Historians differ in their views on the **New Poor Law**. Some criticize it. Others defend and even praise it. Sources D–G are all interpretations by modern historians.

2 Read Sources D–G. Which ones criticize the New Poor Law and which ones support it?

3 a For each of Sources D–G, write down anything in the primary sources which **supports** the view of the modern historian who wrote the source.
   b Also for each of Sources D–G, write down anything in the primary sources which **disagrees** with the view of the modern historian who wrote it.

4 Your answer to question **3** should show that none of the historians who wrote Sources D–G were totally wrong. Yet they clearly disagree with each other. How can this be?

From Pauline Gregg, 'A Social and Economic History of Great Britain', 1950.

7.4 Living Conditions

Between 1801 and 1851 the **population** of Britain doubled from 10.5 million to about 21 million. Industrial towns grew even faster. Manchester's population rose from 75,000 to 450,000. Many towns grew so fast that living conditions became worse.

Overcrowding was one problem. Houses were squeezed into the centres of towns or around the factories (see Source A). Landlords crammed as many people into houses as they could. The 1840 Report on the Health of Towns recorded 39,000 people in Liverpool living in 8,000 one-room cellars under houses.

The **water supply** was another problem. The homes of the poor had no taps. In Highgate, north London, water was bought by the bucketful; at Hyde, near Manchester, people paid a shilling per week to water carriers who brought water in carts; others used standpipes in the street, or local rivers.

Sewage and **rubbish disposal** were also problems. Dirty water, sewage and rubbish might be dumped in the backyard, piled up at the end of the street or thrown into open drains and sewers which ran down the roads. Even where there were drains and sewage pipes, they normally ran into the local rivers – where people collected their water. In London, the Battersea sewer emptied into the Thames just above the Chelsea water intake.

Of course, not everyone lived in the city slums. Country cottages were not so crowded, and water, sewage and rubbish were not such problems there. But the homes of the poor were **cold** and **damp**.

Medical problems

Infectious disease thrived in the towns. In 1840 one in six children died before their first birthday, one in three before they reached 5. **Typhoid** was spread in infected water; **tuberculosis** was carried by bacteria coughed into the air; **typhus** was a virus spread by lice. In 1831 a new killer disease appeared: **cholera** came into Sunderland from abroad. There was an epidemic across the country in 1832. It spread through the water supply. There were further epidemics in 1838, 1848 and 1854. Seven thousand people died of cholera in September 1849 in London alone.

These diseases were worse in towns than in the countryside. They were also worse for the poor than the rich. Wealthier people often had running water in their houses. But since their water supplies were often taken from the infected rivers, even they were not safe.

Source A

An individual wishes to lay out so as to pay him the best percentage in money. He will purchase a plot of ground, then will place as many houses on this acre as he possibly can, without reference to drainage or anything.

From 'The Report on the Health of Towns', 1840, commenting on the motives of house builders.

Source B

19th-century Londoners using the Thames to wash clothes and collect water.

Source C

A 'Punch' cartoonist's view of water from the Thames, 19th century.

Source D

Sheffield in the mid-19th century.

Source E

The water is turned on a certain number of hours a day, four hours perhaps. The poor go to the tap for it. Each person fetches as much as they have pans to receive. It is not sufficient for washing or anything of that kind.

From a report on conditions in Liverpool in the 1840s.

Source F

Shepherd's building consists of two rows of houses with a street between them. In the centre of this street there is a gutter, or more properly sink, into which all sorts of refuse is thrown.

A street in Stockton, Teesside, described in 'The Report on Sanitary Conditions of the Labouring Population', 1842.

Questions

Section A

1 List all of the sources used in this unit. Put them into groups.
   a What types of sources are there?
   b What other types of sources could have been useful?

Section B

2 What do you think the statistics in Source G tell you about life expectancy in England in 1842?

3 What do you think Sources A–F and H tell you about:
   a housing?
   b water supply?
   c disposal of water, sewage and rubbish?

4 The evidence in this unit comes from all kinds of sources. Which do you think are the most valuable to historians?

Source G

Average age of death among different classes		
Class	Rutland (a rural area)	Manchester
professional	52	38
labourers	38	17

From 'The Report on the Sanitary Conditions of the Labouring Population', 1842.

Source H

A painting by Sir Luke Fildes, dated 1874, showing the casualties of London's overcrowding and disease.

7.5 *Public Health*

Nobody seemed to do much about conditions in the towns. Cholera caused a stir in 1832. **Boards of health** were set up in some towns to stop the disease. But as soon as the epidemic passed, these boards were disbanded. Why was progress so slow?

One reason concerned **vested interests**. This was where people had an interest in things staying the same. For example, the water carriers' business would have suffered if there had been fresh water piped into cities.

Another reason was **laissez faire** – the idea that interfering in the private lives of people was none of the government's business. Many people believed this. They argued that what people drank and where they washed or threw their rubbish was their own affair. People who believed this were known as the 'dirty party'!

A third factor was the **cost**. Spending money on drains, sewers, water pipes and rubbish collection would force up taxes and rates. The poor could not afford to pay more. The rich were keen to pay when epidemics were spreading from the slums. But they soon lost interest in better facilities for the poor afterwards.

Slow progress

The turning points were two **official reports**: 'The Sanitary Conditions of the Labouring Population of Great Britain (1842)', organized by **Edwin Chadwick**, and 'The Royal Commission Report on the Health of Towns'. These reports showed people how bad things were and proved the connection between poor living conditions and high death rates. They also showed that private individuals could not be left to solve the problems themselves.

So, as another cholera epidemic raged, the **Public Health Act of 1848** was passed. The Act set up a Central Board of Health. Lord Shaftesbury, Edwin Chadwick and his friend Dr Southwood Smith were members. The board could advise local boards of health or force councils in very unhealthy towns to set one up.

In 1854 the 'dirty party' persuaded Parliament to abolish the Central Board. But Chadwick's work was not forgotten. First came the **Public Health Act of 1875**. This forced all local councils to keep an effective sewage system, clear refuse from the streets and keep pavements lit, paved and clean. Then the **Artisans' Dwellings Act**, also of 1875, allowed councils to clear slums and provide better housing for the poor. In London this resulted in the building of 30,000 new homes.

Source A

The country is sick of centralization, of commissions, of inquiries. The people want to be left to manage their own affairs. They do not want Parliament to be so paternal [fatherly] as it wishes to be – interfering in everybody's business.

George Hudson MP, giving his view in 1847.

Source B

I object also to the Board of Health Commissioners being salaried [paid]. If they have not the patriotism to give their services for the good of the country, they are utterly unworthy of so important a trust.

Colonel Sibthorp MP, objecting to the cost of the Public Health Act proposals in 1847.

Source C

THE COURT OF KING BUMBLE.

A 19th-century cartoon from 'Punch' showing town councils as 'King Bumble', lazy and deaf to the poor.

Better medical treatments

Medical progress helped too. By 1847 **Dr James Simpson** had developed **chloroform** as an **anaesthetic**. Now that surgeons could anaesthetize their patients, they could perform longer and deeper operations. By 1865 **Joseph Lister** had developed **carbolic acid** as an **antiseptic** to prevent surgical wounds becoming infected.

More important as far as infectious diseases were concerned, however, was the work of **Edward Jenner**. In the 1790s he had found that inoculating people with cowpox – a mild and harmless disease – made them immune to **smallpox**. By the 1840s people had overcome their worries about this strange treatment, and the number of deaths from smallpox began to fall.

In the 1860s and 1870s **Louis Pasteur** in France and **Robert Koch** in Germany discovered how to develop **vaccines** to prevent people catching other diseases like diphtheria. Equally important was the improvement in **nursing** in hospitals by methods made popular by **Florence Nightingale**.

A mixture of **new laws** and **medical progress** started to reduce the worst of the health problems in the towns.

Source D

Mr Chadwick and Dr Southwood Smith have been deposed, and we prefer to take our chance with cholera than be bullied into health. There is nothing a man hates so much as being cleansed against his will or having his floor swept, his halls whitewashed, his dungheaps cleared away and his thatch forced to give way to slate. It is a fact that many people have died from a good washing. The truth is that Mr Chadwick has a great many powers, but it is not so easy to say what they can be applied to. Perhaps a retirement pension with nothing to do would be a way of rewarding this gentleman.

Questions

Section A

1 What was the connection between cholera and public health reform?

2 What eventually started to reduce the public health problems in the towns?

Section B

3 It is 1847. The town of Melchester has a serious public health problem. It has thousands of unhealthy, overcrowded homes and a death rate of 45 per 1,000. Cholera has been reported in a nearby town. The town council has called a public meeting to discuss the problem. All kinds of people have arrived – rich, poor, the local MP, water carriers, doctors, factory owners, churchmen, etc.

Write a description of the discussion at the meeting.

◀ *From 'The Times', 1854.*

'Liverpool Quay by Moonlight', painted by John Atkinson Grimshaw in 1887. The air may be a bit murky, but you can see that the streets are paved, cleaned and well lit.
▼

Source E

7.6 Entertainment for All

During the late 19th century, working people were given more time off. It became common for factory workers to be given Saturday afternoon off, and Bank Holidays were introduced in 1871. Many just went to their local pub and drank heavily. Others found new forms of entertainment to fill this increased leisure time – this was long before the days of television and radio. The excellent railway network and cheap fares meant that people could travel more easily. **Day excursions** to the seaside became popular. People were pleased just to get some fresh air into their lungs!

In the industrial towns and cities, **music halls** grew in number. Liverpool and Birmingham had six music halls each and London had 50. There would be a variety of acts including singers, comedians, magicians and acrobats. The audience were quick to show their disapproval if they did not like an act. Music halls were seen as unsuitable for children.

Many of the music-hall **songs** reflected what was happening in the country at the time. For example, the song, 'Goodbye Dolly, I Must Leave You', was first sung during the Boer War of 1899–1902. The audience would join in enthusiastically. The best-loved music-hall singer was **Marie Lloyd**. She was famous for singing 'My Old Man said Follow the Van' and other songs.

Source A

1893 railway poster advertising the seaside resort of Blackpool.

Source B

Barnum and Bailey's Circus entering Bristol in 1897. This famous circus toured the country.

Football teams were often formed by vicars who were anxious to keep the local youths out of trouble on a Saturday afternoon. Everton, Southampton and Aston Villa all started this way. Many others started as works teams, for example, Manchester United and Arsenal. As time went on, games were attended by huge crowds. The 1901 Cup Final was watched by a crowd of 110,000 people.

Source E

The music sheet of the song 'Ta Ra Ra Boom Der-Ay', sung by Lottie Collins in the 1890s. Music sheets were sold so that people could play the song at home. It was a way of making extra money for the performer.

Source C

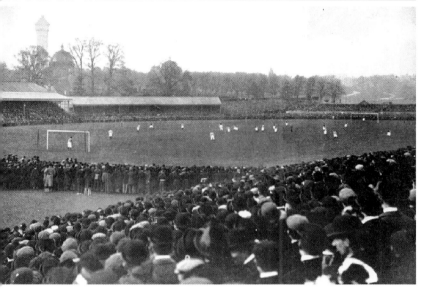

Aston Villa v. Everton at Crystal Palace in 1897. Football became known as 'the people's game'.

Source D

	P	W	D	L	For	Against	Points
						Goals	
Preston North End	22	18	4	0	74	15	40
Aston Villa	22	12	5	5	61	43	29
Wolverhampton Wanderers	22	12	4	6	50	37	28
Blackburn Rovers	22	10	6	6	66	45	26
Bolton Wanderers	22	10	2	10	63	59	22
West Bromwich Albion	22	10	2	10	40	46	22
Accrington	22	6	8	8	48	48	20
Everton	22	9	2	11	35	46	20
Burnley	22	7	3	12	42	62	17
Derby County	22	7	2	13	41	60	16
Notts County	22	5	2	15	39	73	12
Stoke	22	4	4	14	26	51	12

The table at the end of the first Football League season, 1888–9.

Questions

Section A

1 Explain why entertainments like football and the music hall became so popular.

2 Why was the railway so important to the ordinary working person?

Section B

3 How useful is Source A for finding out about leisure in 19th-century Britain? Explain your answer.

4 How useful is Source B for finding out about leisure in 19th-century Britain? Explain your answer.

5 Which is more useful for historians trying to find out about football in the 19th century, Source C or Source D? Give reasons for your answer.

6 Do the sources in this unit prove that life for most people was getting better in the late 19th century?

7.7 Building a Board School

Before 1870 **elementary education** was provided by **voluntary** groups and individuals. The two most important groups were the **National Society** (which provided schools for Church of England children) and the **British and Foreign Society** (which provided schools for Nonconformist children). The government gave an annual grant of money to the two societies.

The government came to realize that these two societies did not have the funds to provide enough schools, and that at least half the children in Britain were receiving no education. It was feared that this would lead to the country falling behind its main industrial rivals, the United States and Germany.

In 1870 **Forster's Education Act** was passed. This said that in areas where there were not enough school places, a **School Board** was to be elected. The boards were given the power to charge local people a rate, buy some land and build a new **board school**. The schools were to be given an annual government grant of money. The amount depended on how well the pupils did in the annual examinations. The Bible was to be taught to children but only in a way acceptable to all Christians, Church of England and others. Attendance between the ages of 5 and 10 was made compulsory in 1880. Even so, many children stayed away from school, often being sent out to work by their parents to bring extra money into the home.

With the coming of the board schools more children received a basic education in reading, writing and arithmetic – the **'three R's'**. This led to the growth of **literacy** and the **popular press**. In 1896 **Lord Northcliffe** started the *Daily Mail*. It catered for the ordinary working person and had large headlines and plenty of photographs.

Itchen Abbas Board School

The 1870 Education Act had a big effect on the Hampshire village of Itchen Abbas. It is possible to reconstruct what happened in the village because several records have survived. They include the **parish vestry minute books**, the **school log books**, the **managers' minutes book** and the **architect's plans** for building the new school. The school was opened in 1875 and is still in use today.

From the managers' minutes book.

Source A

Itchen Abbas. Here is a National school. Nathaniel Bailey, in 1837, left £8 per year on its behalf. Schoolmistress, Miss Frances Warren. Population in 1861 was 214.

From 'Kelly's Trade Directory', 1867.

Source B

Itchen Abbas Rectory
12 April 1873
To the National Society

Dear Sir,
We have been called upon by the government to rebuild our school. We are most anxious to escape being placed under a School Board as the people are all Church of England and desirous of teaching our children this religion. Unfortunately the parish is poor, consisting mainly of farmers and their labourers and without any squire. Under these circumstances I am appealing for a grant from the National Society to enable us to rebuild our school.

I remain faithfully yrs
Rev. W. W. Spicer

From a letter in the National Society Archives. Spicer was trying to get a grant to extend the existing school.

Source C

At a meeting of the ratepayers of Itchen Abbas held at the Rectory on the 10th day of June 1873 it was decided that it was necessary that a School Board should be formed for the said parish of Itchen Abbas.
Signed W. W. Spicer.

Source F

North elevation of Itchen Abbas school as it is today.

Source D

Number of children of school age
in Itchen Abbas:

- **1851** – 31 children
- **1871** – 57 children

From the Census returns.

Source E

*Itchen Abbas School, north elevation. Drawn by
W. H. Hunt, architect, April 1874.*

Source G

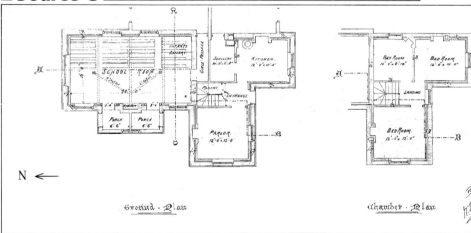

W. H. Hunt's plans, showing the original schoolroom.

Questions

Section A

1 Why was the 1870 Education Act passed?

2 What did it say about the teaching of religion?

3 Why did this Act lead to the growth of the
popular press?

Section B

4 **a** Why was it necessary to build a board school in Itchen Abbas?
 b Was the village in favour of this?
 Give reasons for your answers.

5 What can an historian learn from Sources E and G?

6 **a** If you were investigating how far the school building had changed
 between 1875 and today, which sources in this unit would be the
 most useful? Explain your answer.
 b Would a visit to the school be of any use to you? Give reasons for
 your answer.

8.1 Politics (1): 1700–50

When **Queen Anne** died in 1714, none of her seventeen children were alive to reign after her. Who should be the new monarch? It had to be someone acceptable to Parliament. In 1701 Parliament had passed an Act to make sure the next monarch was a Protestant. The throne passed to George, the ruler of Hanover in Germany. He was the great-grandson of James I and son of Sophia, an English princess who had married abroad.

Long before, when Henry VIII was king in the 16th century, he took little notice of Parliament. He ruled the country with his advisers as it suited him. But King George I had to share power with Parliament.

George I could make policies and choose his own ministers. In particular, he decided which countries England should be friendly with. But there were important limits to his power. Parliament decided how much money to give the Crown out of taxes. If Parliament did not like some of the plans of the Crown, it could refuse to grant the money.

Source B

Resolved, That it hath been found, by Experience, to be inconsistent with the safety and welfare of this Protestant kingdom, to be governed by a Catholic prince.

From the House of Commons resolutions of January 1689.

Source A

A 19th-century portrait of Queen Anne, the last of the Stuart monarchs.

Parliament was different from that of today in many ways. The **House of Lords** was much more powerful then. Most of the important ministers were from the House of Lords. The members of the **House of Commons** were elected, but unlike today, they were not paid. This meant that only wealthy men could serve as Members of Parliament. Like the House of Lords, the Commons was dominated by landowners.

George I was already 54 when he succeeded to the throne. He could not speak English very well and found it difficult to understand English laws and customs. William and Anne had gathered a group of ministers together to discuss important problems and decide policies. George did the same but he soon stopped attending these meetings. Instead, these ministers would make decisions on their own and ask the king for his approval. This group of ministers became known as the **cabinet**. By the reign of George II (1727–60) the cabinet had taken many responsibilities from the Crown.

During this time, the role of **prime minister** first emerged. In cabinet discussions it was natural for one person to take the lead. Although the title was not used at the time, **Sir Robert Walpole** was the 'prime', or first, minister from 1721 to 1742. He had the ability to get people to do what he wanted, and his decisions were rarely challenged by the king.

Source E

Sir Robert Walpole ('prime minister' 1721–42).

Source C

The Lords Spiritual and Temporal and Commons being now assembled in a full and free representation of this nation do in the first place declare: That the pretended power of suspending of laws or the execution of laws by regal authority, as it hath been assumed and exercised of late, is illegal.

From the Bill of Rights, 1689.

Source D

We, your Majesty's most dutiful and loyal subjects the Lords Spiritual and Temporal and Commons in his present Parliament assembled, do beseech your Majesty that it may be enacted and declared that the most excellent Princess Sophia be next in succession in the Protestant line to the imperial crown and dignity of the said realms of England, France and Ireland.

From the Act of Settlement, 1701. This Act made sure that the throne would pass to a Protestant after the death of Queen Anne.

Questions

Section A

1 How do Sources B and D help to explain why George I became King of England after Anne?

2 How was the power of the Crown challenged by the Bill of Rights (Source C)?

Section B

3 **a** Make a list of the ways in which the position and powers of the Crown had changed by the reign of George II when compared to:
  ● 1689
  ● Tudor times.
  b Were there ways in which the position and powers of the Crown were still the same?

8.2 *England and Scotland*

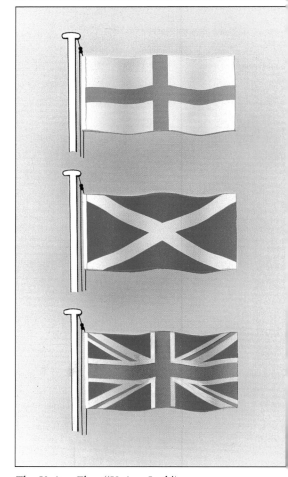

The Union Flag ('Union Jack').

In 1700 the **English** and the **Scots** had little in common and thought of each other as foreigners. They had shared the same monarch since 1603, but they had separate parliaments and different systems of religion, law and education. Scotland was much poorer than England and thousands died of starvation every year if the harvest failed. England's traditional enemy was France, which had a long-standing friendship with Scotland. There was always the threat of invasion of England by the Scots.

Many, however, believed that both countries had more to gain from closer co-operation. England could feel safe from attack; Scotland could share in the rich trade England had with its colonies abroad. Discussions took place between representatives of the two sides. Eventually, it was decided that the two countries should unite. By the **Act of Union, 1707**, England and Scotland became **Great Britain**. There would be one Parliament with representatives from Scotland and England. They would use the same currency and pay the same taxes. Scottish merchants could now trade freely with England and its colonies. It was decided that the churches and the legal and education systems were so different that they should remain separate, as they still are today.

Not everyone was happy with the new arrangement. Many Scots had been unhappy in 1688 when **James II** was forced from his throne. His supporters still thought of him as the rightful king. They were known to offer toasts to 'the king across the water'. Given the opportunity, they would support moves to restore him or his Stuart descendants to the throne. These supporters were known as **Jacobites**, from the Latin for James, *Jacobus*.

There were Jacobites in England as well as Scotland, but support was more widespread in the Highlands. When news of the Union reached the north there were demonstrations and riots against it in Glasgow and Edinburgh. The best chance the Jacobites had was to rise in support of James in Scotland and march south with an army to reclaim the throne.

In 1715 **Queen Anne** was succeeded by **George of Hanover**. It was not certain that he would be popular with the English people. The **Earl of Mar** led a rebellion in Scotland, but it was poorly organized. By the time the son of James II, **James Edward Stuart** (known as the Old Pretender), arrived from France, the Highland armies had broken up and returned to the hills.

Article I That the two kingdoms of England and Scotland shall upon the first day of May which shall be in the year 1707, and for ever after, be united into one kingdom by the name of Great Britain.

Article III That the United Kingdom of Great Britain be represented by one and the same Parliament, to be styled the Parliament of Great Britain.

Article XXII That by virtue of this treaty, of the peers of Scotland sixteen shall be the number to sit and vote in the House of Lords, and forty five the number of the representatives of Scotland in the House of Commons of the Parliament of Great Britain.

Articles of the Act of Union with Scotland, 1707.

A much more serious Jacobite rebellion broke out in 1745. This time it was led by Charles Edward Stuart, the grandson of James II, known as **Bonny Prince Charlie**. Landing in Scotland, he quickly gathered support and proclaimed his father king. After the defeat of government forces at **Prestonpans**, near Edinburgh, he continued the march south into England. Charles hoped that his army of Highland clans would be joined by English Jacobites, but he was to be disappointed. By the time he reached Derby only 300 had joined him and he was having difficulty holding his army together. The decision was taken to turn back.

The **Duke of Cumberland**, the son of George II, was determined to chase the Jacobites into Scotland. What was left of Prince Charles's army was massacred at the **Battle of Culloden** in April 1746. The battle is remembered for the savage way in which the rebels were put to the sword or hanged. Charles managed to escape to France, but the Jacobite cause was dead. The thrones of England and Scotland would stay in the hands of a Protestant.

In time the Scots gained **benefits** from the Union with England. Roads were built, farming improved and, most importantly, living standards were improved by the increase in trade. As a result, industry developed and provided more jobs. More and more Scottish people came to England to make their mark. By the end of the century there was much more understanding between the two countries. However, there was a **price** to pay for this. The whole way of life of the Highland clans was deliberately destroyed by the English after the Battle of Culloden.

Questions

Section A

1 Why might some Scots have been against Union in 1707?

2 Why might some Scots have been in favour of Union in 1707?

3 What reasons might the English have had for uniting with Scotland?

Section B

4 Are Sources A and B evidence that the Scottish people accepted Union with England? Explain your answer.

5 How useful is Source C as evidence of the character and personality of Bonny Prince Charlie?

6 Source C is an artist's impression. Sources D and E are primary written sources. Are they more useful than Source C for a study of Bonny Prince Charlie?

7 Sources D and E disagree with each other over Bonny Prince Charlie's actions at Culloden. Suggest reasons why they disagree.

Source C

Bonny Prince Charlie (1720–88), the 'Young Pretender'.

Source D

The Prince placed himself about the centre, to give orders conveniently. The enemy's canon fire caused much damage. One of the Prince's servants was killed at his side. At the end the Prince did all he could to rally his men, but he was finally obliged to retreat.

Lumsden, Charles's secretary, writing about the Battle of Culloden, 1746.

Source E

The Prince was behind the rear guards. As soon as the left wing gave way, he turned his horse and went off. He never offered to rally his troops.

Elcho, Charles's general, writing about the Battle of Culloden, 1746.

8.3 England and Ireland, 1688–1750

When **James II** came to the throne in 1685 he tried to bring back the Catholic religion. England was a Protestant country, but most people in Ireland were still Catholics. The events of the next few years are some of the most dramatic in Ireland's history – they are remembered in Ireland to this day.

James was deposed in 1688 and fled to France. With French help he landed in Ireland in an attempt to regain his throne. With his army outside the city of **Derry**, the gates of the city were slammed shut. The siege lasted for nearly nine months; many Protestant defenders died of starvation, but they refused to surrender.

William of Orange had replaced James as king and become William III. He arrived in Ireland to put an end to James's plans. His army relieved the city of Derry and went on to defeat James in two further battles at the **River Boyne** and **Aughrim**. The Catholic cause was lost. Ireland was to be kept firmly in the grip of England and the small Protestant Irish minority.

Laws were introduced to make it difficult for Catholics to practise their religion, hold positions of power or own land. Most Catholics scraped a living from the land as tenants of Protestant landlords. They lived in poor hovels and faced eviction if they failed to pay their rent. There were many thousands of wandering beggars.

_ Source B

Catholics could not sit in Parliament, bear arms, own a horse worth more than £5, become apprentice to a gunsmith, hold any army or naval commission, keep a school at home, get education abroad or, from 1727, vote in a parliamentary election.

From Paul Johnson, 'Ireland: Land of Troubles', 1980. Johnson is describing the penal laws.

_ Source C

To the glorious memory of King William III, who saved us from slaves and slavery, knaves and knavery, popes and popery. Whoever denies this toast may be crammed and jammed into the great gun of Athlone and fired into the Pope's belly, and the Pope into the Devil's belly and the Devil into hell, and the door locked and the key in an Orangeman's pocket.

An Orange Order toast, from the early 1800s.

_ Source A

A Protestant wall painting in Ulster from the 1970s.

Poverty was partly the result of the control that England had over Ireland. There was an Irish parliament in Dublin but it had little power. The real ruler of Ireland was the Lord Lieutenant who was appointed from England. Trade was regulated so that there could be no competition with English goods. The Irish were not allowed to export woollen cloth, cattle, sheep, butter or cheese to England or to the British colonies abroad. Only in one county, **Ulster**, where most of the Protestants lived, was there any prosperity. The linen industry developed around Belfast because there was no linen industry in England to compete against it.

Source D

One friend looks at another, and sees his misery, but cannot prevent a lingering death. We cannot feed ourselves with such scraps and morsels as we formerly allowed to our dogs. Nevertheless God has made us this day a defence city and an iron pillar and brazen walls against the whole land.

A sermon preached during the siege of Derry, 1689.

Source E

The separate communities were divided not only by religion but by race and, not least, by culture. They learned different poetry, sang different songs, celebrated different victories, mourned different calamities and, above all, swore different oaths.

From Paul Johnson, 'Ireland: Land of Troubles', 1980.

Source F

A Catholic peasant cottage in the 18th century.

Questions

Section A

1 Copy out the following sentences. Match up each 'head' with the correct 'tail'.

Heads	*Tails*
James II was popular with many people in Ireland	there were new laws to stop Catholics becoming too powerful.
This meant Ireland was	except the area around Belfast.
After James was defeated	because he was a Catholic.
All of Ireland was fairly poor because it could not compete with English trade	a good place to start his fight to get back his throne.

2 How do you think Catholics in Ireland today feel about the victories of William III at the Boyne and Aughrim?

3 Why do you think the penal laws (Source B) were introduced against the Catholics?

4 Why did so many Catholics become poor peasants?

5 How does Source A explain the importance to Protestants of the victory of William III over James II?

Section B

6 Study Source C carefully. Does it provide factual evidence or a point of view? Explain your answer.

7 Imagine you are an Irish Protestant. Which sources would you choose to show pride in your ancestors? Explain your choice.

8 Imagine you are an Irish Catholic. Which sources would you choose to show that your ancestors were badly treated? Explain your choice.

9 Explain why Catholics and Protestants today might look differently upon the events described in this unit.

8.4 Politics (2): 1750 to the 1840s

During the reign of **George III** (1760–1820), Parliament had no organized parties like the ones we have today. There were groups in Parliament led by able men who could rely on the support of their families and friends. The king could choose any of these groups to form a government as long as it could keep the support of Parliament. This gave the **monarch** an influence over policies.

The need for change

Then, as now, there was no voting for the **House of Lords**. It consisted of the aristocracy – the most powerful landowners – and some bishops. There were elections for the **House of Commons**, but the voting system had hardly changed for 200 years.

There was no logic to the places that had MPs. Manchester and Birmingham were becoming huge cities – they didn't have their own MP. Old Sarum was just a grassy mound where there had once been a village – it had two MPs. There was also no logic to who could vote. In some places, for example Preston, all men aged over 21 could vote. In others, the vote went just to people who owned certain houses or were on the borough council. This meant that there were thousands of voters in some places, and very few in others. In Gatton, Surrey, for example, there was only one voter.

There was no **secret ballot** either. People had to say openly who they were voting for. Many **landowners** could threaten so many voters with the sack or eviction that they really controlled the vote on their own. Overall, about one man in ten had the vote – no women voted.

Source A

Stocking workers formed groups that were led, it was said, by a certain Ned Ludd, or King Ludd, from Sherwood Forest. The leader may have been mythical [not a real person], but their actions were practical. They smashed up wide shearing frames used to replace their handlooms. The success of Luddites in Nottinghamshire inspired workers in Lancashire and Cheshire, where steam-powered looms were attacked.

From D. Richards and J. Hunt, 'Modern Britain 1783–1964', 1964.

Source B

Information has reached me that you have those detestable shearing frames and I am desired by my men to write to you and give you fair warning to pull them down. If they are not, I will detach 300 men to destroy them, murder you and burn all your housing.
Signed by the General of the Army of Redressers,
Ned Ludd

A letter sent to a Huddersfield manufacturer in 1812. Letters like this became common in many counties where textile workers were suffering.

Source C

The name 'Luddites' was first used in 1811. John Blackner, an historian, suggested one interpretation. He suggested that 'The frame-breakers assumed the name from an ignorant youth called Ludlam who, when asked by his father to square his needles, took a hammer and beat them into a heap.'

From Malcolm I. Thomis, 'The Luddites', 1970.

Source D

A cartoon drawn by Cruikshank in 1819, showing the government's view of reformers.

Source E

> Sir
>
> This is to acquaint you that if your thrashing Machines are not destroyed by you directly we shall commence our labours
>
> signed on behalf of the whole
>
> Swing

In 1830 there was a depression in farming; wages were low, work was in short supply. Rioting broke out in southern counties. The favourite target was the steam-powered threshing machine which did the work of many men. Many attackers claimed to be led by a mysterious figure called Captain Swing. This letter was sent to a Kent farmer in 1830.

Pressure for change

Society changed during George III's reign. There were changes in agriculture, industry, trade, transport, population, working conditions and living conditions. People could see that the old political system didn't fit this new society. The **landowners** could no longer expect to dominate everyone else. The **middle-class** factory and mine owners were successful and wealthy. They wanted a bigger say in the way Britain was run. The **working classes**, clustered together in huge numbers in towns and factories, demanded a system which did more for them.

These demands from the working people took many forms. Some were demands for political reform; others were more like desperate cries for help. When hard times and machines took away jobs, there were outbreaks of machine-breaking by the **Luddites** and in the **Swing Riots**.

Sometimes the workers joined the middle classes in peaceful demands for **parliamentary reform**. This happened in 1819 when a mass meeting was held in St Peter's Fields, Manchester. It was to be non-violent. Thousands of men, women and children came with banners flying. Halfway through, the magistrates decided that the meeting was illegal and sent a troop of cavalry in to arrest **Orator Hunt**, the main speaker. Angry protesters barred the way. Sabres were drawn; there was general panic. In ten minutes the field was cleared, but 400 people, including 113 women, were wounded and 11 killed. People called it '**Peterloo**', a reference to the Battle of Waterloo of 1815.

Parliament congratulated the magistrates. It was afraid of a British uprising like the French Revolution of 1789. All unrest was crushed. In the Swing Riots of 1830, when poor farm labourers attacked machinery, there was only one death. But nine of the rioters were hanged, 457 transported and over 400 imprisoned.

Source F

MANCHESTER HEROES

A 19th-century cartoonist's view of 'Peterloo'.

Source G

The Act is an historical landmark. It shifted the balance of political power from the South to the Midlands and the North and transferred power from the aristocracy to the urban upper and middle classes. As a banker observed, from now on 'The field of coal would beat the field of barley'.

From P. J. Helm, 'Modern British History', 1965.

Source H

A political revolution had been achieved, and the whole basis of the constitution had been altered. The power of the landlord had been broken.

From R. J. Evans, 'The Victorian Age', 1950.

The year of 1830 was a turning point. **George IV**, who had been against reform, died. **William IV** became king. He dismissed the Tory government that had resisted reform. A Whig government was formed. The Whigs (who later became the Liberal Party) came from a landowning background just like the Tories. But some of their leaders, like **Lord Grey** and **Lord Russell**, believed that reform was necessary. They had been frightened by the Swing Riots. If Parliament did not show that it was willing to reform, they thought, the people would rise up in revolution.

The Great Reform Act

The Whigs persuaded Parliament to pass the **1832 Reform Act**, sometimes called the Great Reform Act. Some people see this Act as the start of democracy in Britain. It changed the way the House of Commons was elected. There was a terrific struggle to get the Act passed. At one stage, when it looked as if it would be rejected, there were riots on the streets of London. But eventually it was passed.

Under the Act, 56 very small places lost the right to elect their own MPs. Thirty other small places lost one of their MPs. London and other large towns and cities were given more MPs. There was to be a single system to decide who could vote. This was based on wealth. In general terms, it was the middle classes who were given the vote. The number of voters increased from 435,000 to 652,000. But there was still no secret ballot; only one man in seven voted; and there were still no votes for women.

After the Act

The reformed Parliament certainly passed more reforms than before. Some of them are shown below. Some benefited the working classes. The **grant to education** in 1833 was only £20,000 per year, but it did help to provide schools for the poor. Workers benefited from the **controls on working conditions** in the mines and factories. But some of the reforms harmed the working classes. They hated the **New Poor Law**, for example.

The middle classes gained most. Middle-class businessmen liked the reorganization of the **banks** and **railways**. The **Municipal Corporations Act** gave them the vote in elections for town councils. The New Poor Law kept the cost to ratepayers low. The Repeal of the **Corn Laws** helped trade.

The king and the landed classes had passed the Reform Act. But it reduced their power. The middle classes had joined the electorate. This gave them more influence. The House of Commons was now the place that reflected the views of the people more. This gave it more influence. The king and the House of Lords began to take second place to the House of Commons.

Source I

An artist's interpretation of the 1832 Reform Act. It shows the people cheering as Britannia kills the old corrupt system, and the Tories against change are sent packing.

Questions

Section A

1 What do you think happened to the political power of the following people between 1750 and the 1840s:
- the monarchy
- the middle classes
- the landowning classes
- the working classes?

Section B

2 Source A says that Ned Ludd **may** have existed. Source C suggests that he didn't. How do you explain this?

3 In writing about Peterloo (page 113), we decided to say that 'Parliament congratulated the magistrates. It was afraid of a British uprising like the French Revolution of 1793.' Source D persuaded us to write this. Can you explain why?

4 'The year of 1830 was a turning point.' Is this **fact** or **opinion**? What do you think are the strengths of this statement?

5 The 1832 Reform Act has been called the Great Reform Act and has been seen as 'the start of democracy in Britain'. Sources G and H are interpretations which support these views. Do you think that the Act deserves such claims? Explain your answer.

1846 REPEAL OF THE CORN LAWS

1842 MINES ACT

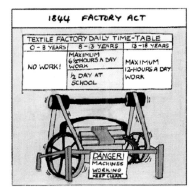

1844 FACTORY ACT

1844 BANK CHARTER ACT

1844 RAILWAY PASSENGERS' ACT

8.5 *The British Empire*

America In 1750 Britain owned thirteen colonies on the east coast of North America. But the colonists didn't see why they should pay taxes to a British Parliament which they had no say in electing. Fighting broke out between the colonists and the British army in 1775. The colonists declared independence in 1776. With the help of France and Spain, the colonists defeated the British. Britain admitted defeat in 1783.

Canada In 1759 **General James Wolfe** captured the French fortress of Quebec and a British colony grew up there. Many people emigrated to Canada, despite the ten-week ocean voyage. Canada's population grew to 3 million by 1865. Its prosperity was based on cattle and wheat production. In 1867 Britain agreed to grant more freedom. The **Dominion of Canada** was created, with its capital at Ottawa.

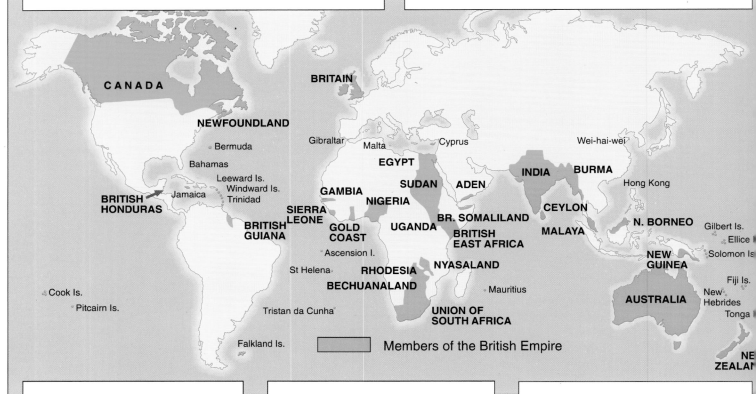

Africa In 1850 Britain's only main interests in Africa were **Cape Colony** and **Egypt**. But between 1880 and 1900, 80 per cent of Africa was divided up among the European powers. Britain took over control of **sixteen colonies.** Between 1899 and 1902 Britain fought the Boer War to take over complete control of South Africa.

India In 1750 the **British East India Company** had trading outposts in places like Madras and Bombay. It used its private army to gain land for Britain. In 1757, for example, **Robert Clive** won the Battle of Plassey to conquer Bengal. Later, the government expanded the British territory. Despite the **Indian Mutiny**, an uprising in 1857, Britain ruled most of India by 1900.

Australia and New Zealand
Captain Cook reached Australia in 1770. It was used as a convict colony from 1788. Sheep farming prospered and **emigration** there increased. Gold was found in 1851. The population grew to 5 million in 1914. **New Zealand** became a British colony in 1840. Farming prospered, especially after refrigeration allowed exports to Europe.

Reasons

One reason for the creation of the British Empire was **trade**. The Industrial Revolution created a need for raw materials such as cotton. It also created wealth and therefore a demand for luxury imports like spices. Manufacturers also needed places where they could sell their goods abroad. Colonies could provide all of these things. In the 18th century, trading companies used their private armies to take land from local rulers; this was what happened in India. In the 19th century it was more often the government which took over territory to prevent other countries like France and Germany getting it first. This was what happened in Africa and New Zealand.

But there were other reasons. The government sometimes took over areas for their **strategic** value. Some British **missionaries** also thought they were 'civilizing' the native peoples. At first the British public were not much interested in the idea of an empire. It wasn't until about 1870 that **imperialism** – enthusiasm for empire – became common among ordinary people in Britain.

Results

What were the results of all this empire building? It did have **trading benefits**. **Imports** from the colonies were more important than the **exports** they bought. Raw materials like muslin, jute, rubber and palm oil flooded in for British industry to use. Exotic products like silk, gold and tea also became available for the British public. There were sometimes also **economic costs**. For example, meat and wool from Australia and New Zealand, and wheat from Canada, were severe **competition** for British farmers by 1900.

In some ways the **colonies benefited** too. The British built roads, canals, railways, schools and hospitals. They also took their medical knowledge, legal system and postal service abroad with them. Some colonies became centres of Christianity. The colonies inherited British laws, language and customs. This was not always welcome, however. Sometimes the **cost to the colonies** was too high. The British rulers often had little respect for local customs, culture and religions. Their ignoring of local attitudes triggered off the **Indian Mutiny**. Local labour was often exploited – slavery lasted until 1833. Native lands were seized. Mass killings sometimes took place. In New Zealand wars and disease reduced the Maori population from about 100,000 in 1815 to 35,000 by 1900.

A poster issued in 1829 by the Governor of Tasmania. It showed the same justice applied for all law-breakers, black or white. However, by 1876 the native black race had been wiped out.

Questions

Section A

1 List the areas that belonged to the British Empire by 1900.

Section B

2 Part of the process of creating the British Empire was **economic**; it was to do with trade. Part of the process was **political**; it was to do with landownership and power. Part of the process was **social**; it was to do with people and their lives.
  a Describe the economic aspects of the British Empire.
  b Describe the political aspects.
  c Describe the social aspects.

3 The three aspects discussed in question **2** were not separate. Describe the ways in which they were linked.

Source A

GOVERNOR DAVEY'S
PROCLAMATION
TO THE ABORIGINES
1816.

8.6 Slavery and the Triangular Trade

During the 18th century Britain was involved in the **slave trade**. Ships left Liverpool and Bristol laden with metal products (chains, iron bars, kettles, pans and pewter plates). They sailed to West Africa where the goods were exchanged for **slaves**.

The slaves were captured from local villages and held in cages until a slave ship arrived. Then the slaves were chained up and packed tightly into the ships, which took them across the Atlantic Ocean to the West Indian islands and America. Because of the filthy conditions on board the ships, many did not survive the journey. Those who did survive were publicly auctioned to the owners of sugar and cotton plantations.

Finally the ships returned to Britain with cargoes of American and Caribbean tobacco, sugar, rum and cotton.

The **triangular voyage** took a year. This inhumane trade brought great wealth to the merchants and ports involved. Many of the merchants bought their way into Parliament so they could make sure their interests were protected.

Plenty of British people supported the slave trade, but others were outraged by it. In 1787 the MP for Hull, **William Wilberforce**, formed the **Society for the Abolition of the Slave Trade**. The society was made up of evangelical Christians. It took until 1807 for Parliament to pass an Act abolishing the slave trade. The Act made it illegal for British ships to carry slaves. But the Act did not give freedom for slaves already working on plantations in British colonies – this did not happen until 1833.

Source A

BARBARITIES in the WEST INDIES

Source B

Many traders sincerely believed that they were helping the Negroes by giving them the chance to become Christians and to escape from the primitive life in the 'dark continent' of Africa.

From R. J. Cootes, 'Britain since 1700', 1968.

Source C

How could the slave trade have happened? Much was simply due to ignorance and lack of understanding – the House of Commons was a long way from West Africa. Very few people in Britain had seen a slave ship, except perhaps as just another sail in the crowded harbours of Bristol and Liverpool.

From Edward Grierson, 'The Imperial Dream', 1972.

Source D

Wilberforce spoke at meetings all over the country. He wanted people to know what went on. He brought models of slave ships, thumbscrews, handcuffs and leg irons. All this brought home to people the inhumanity of the trade.

From A. M. Newth, 'Britain and the World 1789–1901', 1967.

Source E

The anti-slavery movement met dogged opposition from the slave traders who were well represented in Parliament. They argued that conditions for the slaves on the plantations were better than those in their native countries. The slaves kept down the price of sugar and cotton.

From David Taylor, 'Mastering Economic and Social History', 1988.

A cartoon drawn in 1797.

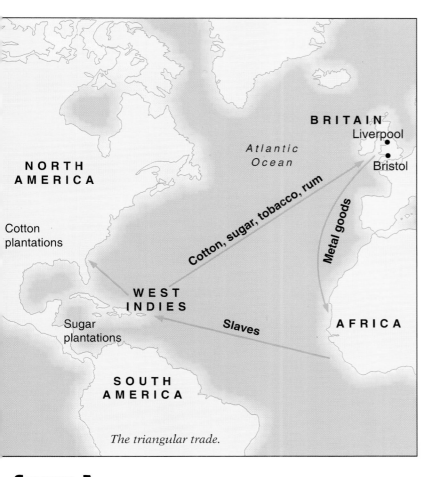

The triangular trade.

Questions

Section A

1 a Copy the map showing the triangular trade.

b Explain what were the **imports** and what were the **exports** of each of the three points of the triangle.

2 a Explain the importance of each of these years in the fight against slavery:
- 1787
- 1807
- 1833.

b Which of these years was the most important in the fight against slavery?

Section B

3 What arguments were used to support the slave trade?

4 Which of the sources in this unit is the most useful for finding out about the conditions in which slaves lived and worked?

5 Source A is a cartoon. Cartoonists often set out to amuse people. Does this make it a useless source? Give reasons for your answer.

Source F

A 19th-century engraving by a British artist. It shows a West Indian plantation before slavery was ended.

8.7 Trade and the Corn Laws

Britain's trading policy, 1750–1900

1750   Britain followed a policy of protection. Duties were so high that smuggling was rife.

1776   Adam Smith wrote **The Wealth of Nations**. He argued that countries should trade freely. This would make them richer in the long run. This book fitted in well with the idea of **laissez faire**, the belief that governments should not interfere with people's lives.

1783   William Pitt, the prime minister, started to get rid of some customs duties.

1815   The first Corn Law was passed.

1823   William Huskisson got rid of more customs duties but not the Corn Laws.

1846   Peel repealed the Corn Laws.

1860   William Gladstone removed all remaining customs duties. Britain was now a free trade nation. At this time Britain was the 'workshop of the world' – with no major competitors – and very prosperous.

1881   The United States and Germany were now serious industrial rivals. Both countries charged duties on British goods. Many people argued that this was not fair and that Britain should return to protection. The factory workers were against this as it would put up the price of food.

1900   Whether or not to keep to free trade was the biggest issue of the day.

During the French Wars (1793–1815), British farmers had received high prices for their corn. They wanted to make sure that this continued during peacetime. So, in 1815 Parliament passed the **Corn Laws**. The Corn Laws said that **no foreign corn could enter Britain unless the price of British corn was £4 per quarter or more**. The Corn Laws, therefore, **protected** British farmers from foreign competition.

Ordinary people hated the Corn Laws for forcing up food prices and wanted them removed; but they had no voice in Parliament. The strongest opposition came from the **Anti-Corn Law League**. It was formed in 1839 and was led by **Richard Cobden** (MP for Stockport) and **John Bright** (MP for Durham). Most of its members were factory owners, so the league had plenty of money. It published leaflets, booklets and posters to put across its point of view. Cobden and Bright travelled the country by train, making speeches at public meetings.

Despite this pressure, nothing was done by Parliament. The Tory prime minister, **Robert Peel**, was sympathetic to the arguments of the League. He believed that trade should flow **freely** between countries. He had, in fact, made it easier and cheaper for foreign industrial products to come into Britain. Most of the Tory Party, however, supported the farmers. If Peel pushed for the **repeal** (abolition) of the Corn Laws, he would be seen as a traitor to his own party. Which way should he act?

In 1846 Peel was forced to act by events outside his control. The winter of 1845–6 was very wet. The corn harvest in England was a disaster. There was a shortage of corn, and the price of bread went up. In Ireland things were worse. The potato crop – the main food of the Irish people – went rotten. The English did not have any corn to send to Ireland, and there was a famine; over a million people starved to death. Peel decided that the Corn Laws must go at all costs. If they were abolished, foreign corn could come into Britain freely and this would make bread cheaper in England and Ireland.

The Corn Laws were abolished on 26 June 1846. But it was too late to save the Irish from starvation. Most Tory MPs were very annoyed with Peel. He was forced to resign and never held office again.

Source A

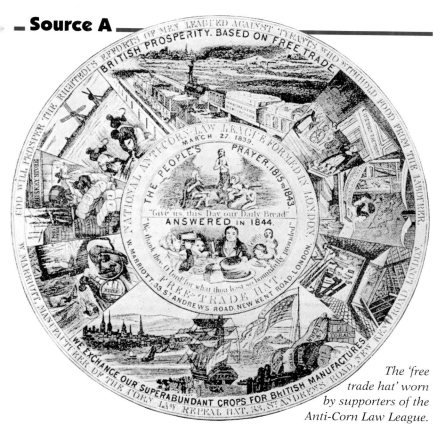

The 'free trade hat' worn by supporters of the Anti-Corn Law League.

Source B

Manufacturers [factory owners] hoped that if the Corn Laws were repealed the price of bread would fall. They also argued that if foreign countries sold their corn to Britain they would have money to buy British goods. This would lead to an expansion of trade and industry.

From Robert Unwin, 'Britain since 1700', 1986.

Source C

Supporters of the Corn Laws argued that the only reason the manufacturers wanted to repeal the Corn Laws was to bring down the price of bread and so lessen demand for higher wages.

From Philip Sauvain, 'British Economic and Social History', 1987.

Source D

The working classes accepted the aims of the Anti-Corn Law League for cheap bread. But they distrusted the middle-class organizers of the League, whom they knew as the employers who gave them long hours and low wages. Bright himself opposed Factory Acts.

From W. D. Hussey, 'British History 1815–1939', 1971.

Source E

THE DEAF POSTILION.
A POLITICAL PARODY, AFTER GEORGE CRUIKSHANK.

A cartoon from 'Punch' in 1846. A 'postilion' rode one of a team of coach-horses to guide the coach.

Questions

Section A

1 What is meant by **protection** and **free trade**?

2 'Source A is biased and therefore useless.' Do you agree? Give reasons for your answer.

3 What point is Source E making? Explain your answer.

Section B

4 The Corn Laws were designed to stop foreign competition. It might have seemed reasonable for all British people to want this. Why, then, did the Corn Laws cause such a lot of argument in Britain in the 1840s?

5 Some history books say that the Anti-Corn Law League was responsible for the repeal of the Corn Laws. Do you agree? Give reasons for your answer.

8.8 Politics (3): the 1840s to 1900

In 1837 **Queen Victoria** came to the throne. It was the start of a new era. But there were no immediate gains for the working classes. The 1832 Reform Act had not given them the vote, and the reformed Parliament did not pass the laws they wanted. Working-class pressure for change continued.

Chartism

Chartism was a working-class movement which pressed for sweeping changes to the electoral system. The Chartists' 'Six Points' made up the 'People's Charter'. Chartism got mass support in times of depression; but when times improved, support fell.

Some Chartist leaders, like **Feargus O'Connor**, wanted to **force** Parliament to accept the Charter. In 1839 about 1,000 Chartists, led by **John Frost**, planned an an uprising in Newport, Wales. Soldiers were used to drive them off. There were plans for a national strike by Chartists in 1842. But workers were too desperate for jobs to risk them by striking. Other leaders, like **William Lovett**, opposed force. They wanted to **persuade** Parliament.

The Chartists collected **petitions** demanding the Charter in 1839, 1842 and 1848. The 1848 petition had 5 million signatures; but it was full of forged names. All the petitions were rejected. The changes demanded were too extreme. Also, the violence of some of the Chartists persuaded both the aristocracy and the middle classes in Parliament to join forces to oppose them.

Source A

THE SIX POINTS OF THE PEOPLE'S CHARTER

A VOTE
for every man of at least 21 years of age.

A SECRET BALLOT
to protect the elector as he votes.

NO PROPERTY QUALIFICATIONS FOR MPs
enabling the return of the man of their choice, rich or poor.

PAYMENT OF MEMBERS
enabling a working man to serve.

EQUAL CONSTITUENCIES
to get fair representation for everyone.

ANNUAL PARLIAMENT
so members, when elected for a year only, would not be able to betray their constituents as now.

A summary of the People's Charter taken from a poster of the time.

Source B

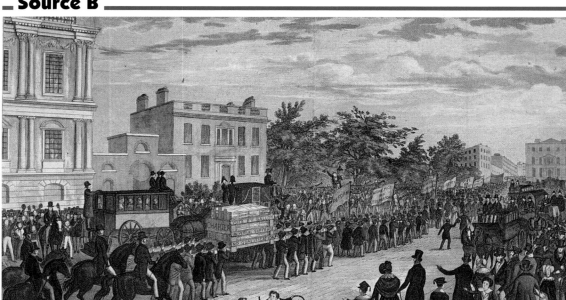

The procession which took the 1842 Chartists' petition to Parliament. It had over 3 million signatures and was rejected in the House of Commons by 287 votes to 49.

New model unions

Trade unions were more effective. The first successful trade unions were the **new model unions**, like the Amalgamated Society of Engineers, formed in 1851. This union had 33,000 members by 1868. These were unions for skilled workers who could afford fairly high subscriptions. This gave them enough income to pay for efficient administration, full-time paid officials and benefits to members. These unions were very moderate. They didn't threaten to destroy industry, but negotiated for improvements within it. There were very few strikes.

The Second Reform Act

The union leaders were based in London. They began to meet politicians to argue that working men should have the vote. Politicians were impressed by their organization and moderation. They began to consider the idea. There was certainly still a need for reform of Parliament. Only one man in six could vote (still no women). The industrial towns had been steadily growing since 1832 and needed more MPs.

New attitudes were gradually developing in Parliament. The aristocracy which had once dominated both parties was now less powerful. Both parties had reorganized to fight elections. The Tories had developed into the Conservative Party, the Whigs into the Liberal Party. Both had a new type of leader – like **William Gladstone**, a Liberal, and **Benjamin Disraeli**, a Conservative – who could see that working people should be given a share of power.

Source C

The union does all it possibly can to prevent any strike. Where they have time and opportunity, they cause a deputation to the workmen to wait on their employers to represent their grievances, and then give advice afterwards. We believe strikes to be a waste of money, not only in relation to the workers but also to the employers.

William Allen, general secretary of the Amalgamated Society of Engineers (ASE), giving the union's view of strikes.

Source D

The weekly subscription to the union was one shilling (= 5p). In return, the union paid sickness and unemployment benefit, pensions and funeral and accident benefits. The amounts paid out by the union in 1865 were:

Unemployment pay	£14,076
Sickness pay	£13,788
Pensions for aged members	£5,184
Funeral benefits paid to members' wives	£4,887
Accident benefits to disabled members	£1,800

A summary of the finances of the ASE in 1865.

Source E

The union card of the ASE. Notice the solid and respectable image it gives.

Source F

Striking dock workers demonstrating on the streets in 1889.

Source G

I do not believe in having sick pay, out-of-work pay or any number of other pays. We desire to prevent sickness and men being out of work. The way to accomplish this is firstly to organize, then reduce your hours of labour, and that will prevent illness and members being out of employment.

Comment by Will Thorne, leader of the Gas Workers' Union, 1889.

Viscount Palmerston, the leader of the Liberals, died in 1865. He had always been against reform. His death made reform easier. In London there was a mass meeting demanding reform. Both parties wanted to get the credit for reform. In 1867 the Tory government decided to move; it passed the **Second Reform Act**.

The Act increased the electorate from 1.35 million to 2.45 million. The new voters were the better-off workers in the towns. Forty-five House of Commons seats were moved from small rural areas to the towns.

After the Second Reform Act

The new electorate produced Parliaments that passed several reforms. Both Gladstone and Disraeli led governments. Some of their reforms are described below. Many of these benefited working people. There was also more reform of Parliament itself. In 1872 the **Ballot Act** was passed. This made voting secret. In 1884 more working people were given the vote. The number of voters rose from about 3 million to about 5 million.

But the population was 30 million, so many adults still did not vote – there was still no vote for women. Many working people were still unhappy with their lives. They needed another way to make their voice heard. This led to a fresh wave of trade unions called **new unions**.

New unions and the Labour Party

The new unions were for **unskilled labourers**, like the dockers. They were different from the new model unions. They had lower subscriptions and paid few benefits. Their policy was to **force** employers to make changes. The dockers' strike forced an increase in pay in 1889. By 1900 there were 2 million members of these unions.

The new unions began to work with the small number of working-class MPs in Parliament, like **Keir Hardie**. In 1900 they

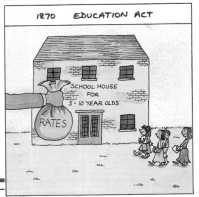

Source H

The House of Commons in the 19th century. The Speaker sat in the centre, the government MPs on the left and the opposition party on the right.

...ormed the **Labour Representation Committee (LRC)** to help ...orking-class candidates for Parliament. In 1903, 29 LRC ...andidates were elected. They decided to call themselves the ...abour Party.

Queen Victoria died in 1901. The monarch and the House of ...ords had become less and less powerful. The middle classes ...ominated the Liberals and the Conservatives. Elections were ...airer, and more people could vote. But many of the working class ...ere still not satisfied. The Labour Party and unions would fight on ...nto the 20th century.

Questions

Section A

1 Design a diagram to show the number of voters before 1832; after 1832; after 1867; after 1884.

2 Draw up a table which compares the **new model unions** and the **new unions**. Use these headings for your table: Date; Members; Subscriptions; Aims; Methods; Successes.

3 What happened to the political power of the working classes during Queen Victoria's reign?

Section B

4 Here is a list of possible reasons why Chartism failed:
   ● support was only strong in times of hardship
   ● leaders were divided over tactics
   ● military force was used against them
   ● strikes were difficult in times of hardship
   ● Parliament was frightened by their violence
   ● there were forgeries on the petition
   ● Parliament rejected the petitions
   a Decide whether these causes are all separate or whether any are linked.
   b Divide the list into types of cause – e.g. economic reasons, political reasons, other reasons; **or** Parliament's actions, Chartists' actions.
   c Decide whether you think some of the causes are more important than others. Make sure you have reasons for your decision.

5 Use the approach in question **4** to explain why the Second Reform Act was passed in 1867.

8.9 England and Ireland 1750–1900

Unit 8.3 explained some of the problems in Ireland. One was **religious**. Three-quarters of the Irish were Catholic. But the British insisted that the Protestant Church should be the official Church in Ireland. They passed laws, like the Test Acts, which prevented Catholics from holding public office or becoming teachers or high-ranking soldiers. Another problem was **economic**. The government controlled landownership. In 1800, Catholics owned only 15 per cent of the land. They had to rent from Protestant (often English) landowners.

These grievances caused frequent unrest in Ireland. In the 1790s, when Britain was at war with the French, an Irish rebellion was led by **Wolfe Tone**. He hoped that the French would distract the English forces. But the revolt failed.

The prime minister at that time was **William Pitt the Younger**. The rebellion made him believe that the only way to make Ireland loyal to Britain was to unite the countries. In 1800 he got Parliament to pass the **Act of Union**. This abolished the Parliament in Dublin and instead gave the Irish 100 MPs and 32 lords at Westminster. Britain and Ireland were now joined together in the **United Kingdom**. Many of the Irish didn't approve of this either. This added a **political** dimension to the problems.

Source A

Every person that shall bear any office, civil or military, in the service of his majesty will take several oaths of allegiance. And all persons that do refuse to take said oaths and Protestant sacrament shall be disabled in law to have the said office.

The Test Act of 1673.

Source B

Such is the extraordinary power of their agitators, that they could lead on the people to open rebellion at a moment's notice. And such is their organization, that I believe their success is inevitable.

The Lord Lieutenant of Ireland reporting on the state of Ireland in 1829.

Source C

A Rowlandson cartoon from 1801. William Pitt, riding the British bull, is seen locked together with St Patrick riding the Irish bull. Pitt seems to believe that things will work out in the end; St Patrick has his doubts. What do you think the artist thought?

Desperate Irish people during the mid-19th-century famine crowd outside a workhouse in the hope of some food.

Pitt had promised the Irish Catholics equal rights with Protestants to get their support for the Act of Union. But **George III** refused to allow this. The Irish were furious. In the 1820s **Daniel O'Connell** started a campaign in Ireland demanding equality. There was a danger of another rebellion. So, despite the opposition of **George IV**, in 1829 the prime minister, the **Duke of Wellington**, got Parliament to pass the **Catholic Emancipation Act**, which gave equality to Catholics.

The next crisis in Ireland was the **famine** of 1845 when the **potato crop** failed. Agriculture had not been developed there; about 2 million people relied on this single crop for food. Potato blight reduced every crop until 1849. Although the British government tried to help, it did not do enough. Shortage of food led to famine and disease. In the end, a million people died and 1.5 million emigrated. The Irish never forgave the British for their failure to prevent these deaths.

In the 1870s poverty returned to Ireland. Imports of cheap food from abroad reduced profits on the land. Again there was unrest. A terrorist group called the **Fenians** started a campaign of violence against the British government. The prime minister at this time was **William Gladstone**. He tried to remove Irish grievances. In 1869 he took away the privileged position of the Protestant Church in Ireland. He also passed two **Land Acts** in 1870 and 1881 to enable the Irish to buy the land they rented.

But this was not enough. The Irish, inspired by **Charles Parnell**, by now wanted independence or, failing that, **Home Rule** – a parliament of their own in Dublin to control domestic affairs. Gladstone tried to get Parliament to agree to this, but the Protestants in Ireland and MPs from both parties in Britain combined to prevent him.

In 1900 Ireland was still under British control. Since then, the south of Ireland has become an independent country, called **Eire** (or the Irish Republic). Northern Ireland is still part of the United Kingdom. But the tensions between England and Ireland and between Catholics and Protestants in Ireland are still severe.

Source D

Source E

The poorer classes reside mainly in separate quarters of one particular faith. In the district of West Belfast, the Shanklin Road is an almost purely Protestant district. The great Catholic district is known as the Falls Road. The land between the two quarters has been the location of some of the worst riots.

An official report on unrest in Belfast, 1886.

Questions

Section A

1 What were the main grievances of the Irish in 1750?

2 How did the Act of Union add to their grievances?

Section B

3 Compare the situation in Ireland in 1801 with the situation by 1900.
 a Had it changed?
 b Had it improved?
 Explain your answers.

4 Read Source E. How much has changed and how much has stayed the same since it was written?

Heinemann Educational,
a division of Heinemann Educational Books Ltd,
Halley Court, Jordan Hill, Oxford OX2 8EJ

OXFORD LONDON EDINBURGH
MADRID ATHENS BOLOGNA PARIS
MELBOURNE SYDNEY AUCKLAND SINGAPORE
TOKYO IBADAN NAIROBI HARARE
GABORONE PORTSMOUTH NH (USA)

© John Child, Tim Hodge, Paul Shuter and David Taylor 1992
The moral rights of the proprietors have been asserted.

First published 1992

British Library Cataloguing in Publication Data is available from
the British Library on request.

ISBN 0 435 31211 1

Designed and produced by Visual Image, Street, Somerset

Originated by Monarch Litho Gravure Ltd, Bristol

Printed and bound in Hong Kong by Mandarin Offset

92 93 94 95 96 11 10 9 8 7 6 5 4 3

Acknowledgements

The authors and publisher would like to thank the following for permission to reproduce photographs:
Ancient Art and Architecture Collection: 1.1F
Ann Ronan Picture Library: 5.11A, 6.5D
Ashmolean Museum: 5.6A
Bettmann Archive, New York: 1.4C
Bodleian Library: 1.1A, 1.1B
Osvaldo Böhm (Galleria Dell Accademia, Venice): 1.1C
Bridgeman Art Library: 1.2B, 1.5B (City of Bristol Museum and Art Gallery), 2.4B, 4.2B, 6.1D, 6.8E, 7.4H, 7.5E, 8.1A, 8.6F
British Film Institute (Colombia Pictures Corporation): 5.4B
British Library: 2.4A, 2.4B, 2.4C, 5.2A, 5.9A, 5.11B, 7.3C
Trustees of the British Museum: 5.1C, 5.8D, 8.4D, 8.6A, 8.9C
Photographie Bulloz: 3.2B
Rex Cathcart: 8.3A
Collections (Brian Shuel): 6.5A, 6.5B
Dean & Chapter of Westminster: 2.2C
C. M. Dixon: 5.5A
E. T. Archive: 6.1F, 8.4F
Fotomas Index: 4.4A, 5.3A, 5.3C, p.60, 5.11A, 5.11D
Photographie Giraudon: Cover
Herzog Anton Ulrich-Museums Braunschweig: 1.3B
Hulton Picture Company: 2.1B, 4.4C, 5.7A, 6.2B, 6.9C, 8.2C, 8.7A
Illustrated London News Picture Library: 6.4C
Institute of Agricultural History and Museum of English Rural Life, University of Reading: 6.1G
Ladybird Books: 6.4D
Mansell Collection: 1.5A, 1.7F, 3.4A, 5.1E, 5.9C, 6.3A, 6.3C, 6.7D, 6.7E, 6.9D, 7.1A, 7.2A, 7.4D, 8.7E, 8.9D
Colin Martin: 4.6E

Mary Evans Picture Library: 4.1B, 4.1C, 6.1H, 6.2D, 6.8A, 7.6C
Musée Cantonal des Beaux-Arts de Lausanne: 3.3E
Museum of London: 5.10C
National Library of Australia (Rex Nan Kivell Collection): 8.5A
National Portrait Gallery: 2.2B, 2.4A, 3.4B, 4.2A, 5.4A, 8.1E
National Railway Museum, York: 6.9A, 6.9E, 7.6A
Private Collection: 4.2D
Punch Publications: 7.4C, 7.5C
E. Richardson (Mander & Mitchenson Collection): 7.6E
Chris Ridgers: 6.7C
Robert Harding Picture Library: 5.10B
Royal Collection, St James's Palace © Her Majesty the Queen: 2.3A
Royal Commission on the Historical Monuments of England: 8.8H
Scala: 1.2D, 1.2E, 1.4D, 3.1A, 3.1D, 3.2C
Scottish National Portrait Gallery: 4.5B; 5.6C (by permission of the Earl of Rosebery)
Staatliche Kunstammlungen, Dresden (Herbert Boswank): 1.5E
Statens Konstmuseer (Swedish Portrait Archives, Gripsholm): 1.7A
David Taylor: 7.7F
Topham Picture Source: 7.1G, 8.4E, 8.8F
Weidenfeld Archives: 8.8B
Reece Winstone: 7.6B

Cover photo: A contemporary water-colour of Elizabeth I's funeral procession.

The authors and publisher would also like to thank the following for permission to reproduce copyright material:
Hampshire County Record Office: 7.7E, 7.7G; R. R. Selman: 4.6C

Every effort has been made to contact copyright holders of material reproduced in this book. Any omissions will be rectified in subsequent printings if notice is given to the publisher.

Details of Written Sources

In some sources the wording or sentence structure has been simplified to ensure that the source is accessible.
Nicholas Bentley, *The Victorian Scene 1837–1901*, Weidenfeld and Nicolson, 1968: 7.3F; Neil Buxton, *The Economic Development of the British Coal Industry*, Batsford Academic, 1978: 6.4E; *Calendar of State Papers, Venetian Series*: 5.1A; Mary Carter, Christopher Culpin, Nicholas Kinloch, *Past into Present 2*, Collins Educational, 1989: 1.1D; *Cassell's Illustrated History of England*, Cassell, 1873: 1.4A; R. J. Cootes, *Britain since 1700*, Longman, 1968: 8.6B; R. J. Cootes, *The Middle Ages*, Longman, 1972: 1.2A; Leonard Cowie, *The Reformation of the Sixteenth Century*, Wayland, 1972: 1.2C, 1.4B, 1.5F, 1.6B, 1.7D, 1.7E, 3.1A, 3.1B, 3.2A, 3.2D, 3.3A, 3.3B, 3.4C, 3.4D, 3.4E; Godfrey Davies, *The Restoration of Charles II*, OUP, 1955: 5.8A; A. G. Dickins, *The Age of Humanism and Reformation*, Longman, 1972: 1.1E, 3.3C, 3.3D; *England's Joy*, 1660: 5.8B; R. J. Evans, *The Victorian Age*, Edward Arnold, 1950: 8.4H; Pauline Gregg, *A Social and Economic History of Great Britain*, Harrap, 1950: 7.3G; Edward Grierson, *The Imperial Dream*, Collins, 1972: 8.6C; P. J. Helm, *Modern British History*, Bell, 1965: 8.4G; Paul Hentzner, *Travels in England in the Reign of Queen Elizabeth*, 1889. In: Schools Council Project: History 13–16, *Elizabethan England*, Holmes MacDougall, 1977: 4.2C; David Howarth, *The Voyage of the Armada: The Spanish Story*, Collins, 1981: 4.6D; John Hunter, *Mary Stuart and John Knox*, Chambers, 1978: 4.5A; W. D. Hussey, *British History 1815–1939*, CUP, 1971: 8.7D; Paul Johnson, *Ireland: Land of Troubles*, Eyre Methuen, 1980: 8.3B; J. A. P. Jones, *The Early Modern World, 1400-1700*, Macmillan, 1979: 4.1A; *Kelly's Trade Directory, 1867*, Hampshire County Library Service, 1867: 7.7A; David Kennedy, *Tudors and Stuarts*, Hutchinson, 1981: 2.2D; H. G. Koenigsberger, G. L. Mosse, *Europe in the Sixteenth Century*, Longman, 1981: 1.3A, 1.7B; Robert Latham, William Matthews (Eds.), *The Diary of Samuel Pepys*, Bell and Hyman, 1971–83: 5.9D, 5.10A; M. H. Lee (Ed.), *Diaries and Letters of Philip Henry*,

1882: 5.6B; John Lynch, *Spain under the Hapsburgs, 1516–1598*, Blackwell, 1964: 4.6B; Hamish MacDonald, *The Irish Question*, Basil Blackwell, 1985: 8.3C, 8.3E; Colin Martin, Geoffrey Parker, *The Spanish Armada*, Guild Publishing, 1988: 4.6F; T. W. Moody, F. X. Martin, F. J. Byrne (Eds.), *A New History of Ireland*, volume III, *Early Modern Ireland 1534–1691*, OUP, 1976: 4.3C; R. Myers, *England in the Late Middle Ages, 1377–1536*, Penguin, 1952: 2.2A; A. M. Newth, *Britain and the World 1789–1901*, Penguin, 1967: 8.6D; David Ogg, *England in the Reign of Charles II*, OUP, 1956: 5.10D; John Patrick, *Waterloo to the Great Exhibition*, John Murray, 1981: 7.3D; M. M. Reese, *Tudors and Stuarts*, Edward Arnold, 1971: 4.1D; *The Reformation*, Reader's Digest, 1974: 1.5C, 1.6A; D. Richards, J. Hunt, *Modern Britain 1783–1964*, Longman, 1950: 8.4A; C. R. N. Routh, *They Saw it Happen, 1485–1688*, Basil Blackwell, 1956: 5.1B; R. N. Rundle, *Britain's Economic and Social Development*, University of London Press, 1973: 6.4B; Philip Sauvain, *British Economic and Social History*, Stanley Thornes, 1987: 8.7C; Schools Council Project: History 13–16, *Medicine Through Time II*, Holmes MacDougall, 1976: 5.9B; Paul Shuter, John Child, David Taylor, *Skills in History Book 2*, Heinemann Educational, 1989: 5.11C; L. E. Snellgrove, *The Early Modern Age*, Longman, 1972: 1.5B, 1.7C; P. F. Speed, *History through Maps and Diagrams: The Industrial Revolution to the Present Day*, Arnold-Wheaton, 1985: 6.4A; Rev. John Stoughton, *The Acts and Monuments of John Foxe*, Religious Tract Society: 2.5C; Susan J. Styles, *The Poor Law*, MacMillan, 1985: 7.3E; David Taylor, *Mastering Economic and Social History*, MacMillan, 1988: 8.6E; Malcolm I. Thomis, *The Luddites, Machine Breaking in Regency England*, David and Charles, 1970: 8.4C; R. J. Unstead, *Crown and Parliament, 1485–1688*, A & C Black, 1962: 4.3A; Robert Unwin, *Britain since 1700*, Hutchinson, 1986: 6.2F, 8.7B; Michael J. Walsh, *The Council of Trent*, Reader's Digest, 1974: 3.1E; Stephen White-Thompson, *Elizabeth I and Tudor England*, Wayland, 1984: 4.6A; Annabel Wigner, *Ireland*, Dryad Press, 1988: 8.3D; Neville Williams, *Elizabeth I*, Weidenfeld and Nicolson, 1972: 4.3B